STOCK MARKET CYCLES

STOCK MARKET CYCLES

A Practical Explanation

STEVEN E. BOLTEN

Q

QUORUM BOOKS
Westport, Connecticut • London

Library of Congress Cataloging-in-Publication Data

Bolten, Steven E.
    Stock market cycles : a practical explanation / Steven E. Bolten.
        p.   cm.
    Includes bibliographical references and index.
    ISBN 1–56720–320–5 (alk. paper)
    1. Stock exchanges.   I. Title.
  HG4551.B485   2000
  332.64'2—dc21   99–046054

British Library Cataloguing in Publication Data is available.

Library of Congress Catalog Card Number: 99–046054
ISBN: 1–56720–320–5

First published in 2000

Quorum Books, 88 Post Road West, Westport, CT 06881
An imprint of Greenwood Publishing Group, Inc.
www.quorumbooks.com

Printed in the United States of America

The paper used in this book complies with the
Permanent Paper Standard issued by the National
Information Standards Organization (Z39.48–1984).

10 9 8 7 6 5 4 3 2

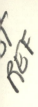

Contents

Acknowledgments

Stock Market Cycles: A Practical Explanation and I are an evolutionary mosaic of experiences, pleasant and not so pleasant lessons, interactions with wonderful people, and many life-shaping events and actions done and yet to be done. I acknowledge them.

My wife, Marjorie; our three children, Brian, Fiona, and Eamon; our dog, Sadie; and a blessed lifetime with wonderful parents are great encouragement.

Early roots of this book trace back to Professors James R. Longstreet and Julius Grodinsky at the Wharton School of Finance and Commerce at the University of Pennsylvania, and the works of John Burr Williams and Myron J. Gordon.

Thought-provoking twists and turns came from Professors Elton, Gruber, Ritter, Carlton, Keenan, and Altman of the Stern Graduate School of Business at New York University. A short stint at Merrill Lynch offered other insights.

Intellectual banter with colleagues at the University of Houston and the University of South Florida provided further stimulating ideas. I remember conversations with R. Charles Moyer, Richard Meyer, Jainping Qi, Bill Francis, Susan Long, Paul Solomon, Greg Marshall, Steve Kapplin, and Eugene Dunham.

Academic and professional organization activities widened my horizons. In various capacities with the Eastern Finance Association, Financial Management Association, and other organizations, I discussed ideas with Ed Moses, Diana Harrington, Robert Schweitzer,

Don Wiggins, Ted Veit, and many others. I also witnessed a myriad of approaches, concepts, techniques and tactics about stock market behavior. The American Society of Appraisers and the Institute of Business Appraisers acquainted me with Ray Miles, Shannon Pratt, Z. Christopher Mercer, Jay Fishman, and James Schilt, and taught me much about valuation.

My coauthors, Scott Besley, Susan W. Long, John Crockett, and Rob Weigand, whose joint efforts appear herein, contributed to my thoughts.

Many journal editors and reviewers provided thought-provoking commentary. I expressly and formally acknowledge the journals and their editors who gave reprint permission for the following articles included herein:

Steven E. Bolten and Yan Wang, "The Impact of Management Depth on Valuation," *Business Valuation Review*, September 1997, pages 143–145.

Steve E. Bolten, "Time Horizon Premiums as a Measure of Stock Market Bubbles," *Business Valuation Review*, September 1999, pages 134–137.

Steven E. Bolten and Robert A. Weigand, "The Generation of Stock Market Cycles," *The Financial Review*, Vol. 33 February (1998), pages 77–84.

Steven E. Bolten and Susan W. Long, "A Note on Cyclical and Dynamic Aspects of Stock Market Price Cycles," *The Financial Review*, Vol. 21, No. 1, February 1986, pages 145–149.

Steven E. Bolten and Scott Besley, "Long-Term Asset Allocation under Dynamic Interaction of Earnings and Interest Rates," *The Financial Review*, Vol. 26, No. 2, May 1991, pages 269–274.

Steven E. Bolten and John H. Crockett, "The Influence of Liquidity Services on Beta," *Review of Financial Economics* (formerly *The Review of Business and Economic Research*), Vol. 13, No. 3, April 1978, pages 38–49.

Steven E. Bolten, "A Note on the Price Earnings Multiple," *Valuation* (March 1991): 128–131. Reprinted by permission of the American Society of Appraisers.

1

Introduction

"Security prices will fluctuate," is the classic quote attributed to J. P. Morgan when asked what the stock market would do. He was right, of course. Why? "Supply and demand," the first-year finance student answers. The student is also right, of course. Why?

Investors need look no further than the reported annual stock price range in any financial publication to observe that stock prices fluctuate. The yearly high is considerably higher than the yearly low. Why?

Is there a conceptual framework underlying the fluctuations? Does supply and demand shift in reaction to basic, underlying causes that can be identified? Is there a generally consistent and repetitive interaction among the causes? Can this framework skeleton be perceived repeatedly through all the noise and emotion associated over the centuries with stock markets and financial asset pricing?

THE CONCEPT OF COMMON STOCK VALUE

What gives a piece of paper, known as common stock, value? What makes an investor exchange cash, which can be used to purchase almost anything, for a share of common stock, which in and of itself can purchase nothing? The physical stock certificate has no purchasing power. There must be some expected reward or future benefit that will entice investors to part with their money in exchange for the stock certificate.

Exactly what does the investor get by buying the share of common stock? The answer is obvious. The investor acquires a claim on all future benefits that are transferred from the corporation to the investor. The only benefit that can be transferred from the corporation to the investor is distributions, usually cash dividends. Stockholders rarely receive physical assets, such as a corporate-owned car or plant, from the corporation.

The motivation to purchase a share of common stock is the expectation of a return high enough to warrant undertaking the risk associated with the ownership of that particular share of common stock. The motivation to sell the share is the expectation of a rate of return no longer high enough to warrant undertaking the risk associated with the ownership of that particular share of common stock. The relationship between the expected rate of return and risk changes, motivating investors to purchase or sell the share.

Skeptics respond that the share of common stock can be purchased for capital-gain potential in addition to future dividends. The price at which the common stock may be sold in the future is always a function of the claim on future benefits, namely dividends, expected to be received by the new purchaser. A corporation that will never, with iron-clad certainty, distribute any of its earnings or assets to its stockholders must, with certainty, have a common stock that has no value other than the piece of paper on which it is printed. Most stock certificates are not works of art and, therefore, have no value as a piece of paper.

EXPECTED RATE OF RETURN VS. RISK

The expected return must compensate investors for the risk associated with purchasing a particular share of common stock or investors will not buy the share, or if already owned, will sell it. Different company common shares may be compared on an expected return/ risk basis. The most attractive shares are those with the highest expected rate of return for the risk or the lowest risk for the expected rate of return.

The common shares of different companies compete for investors' limited funds on this expected rate of return/risk basis. Investors continually seek the most attractive expected rate of return/risk relationships and continually adjust their common stock portfolios by exchanging among common stocks and/or between other categories of assets. This equilibrating process is typically called "fungibility," the exchanging among competing shares and other assets by investors in search of the most attractive expected rate of return/risk relationships. The concept of fungibility is applicable to all financial assets, particularly among publicly-traded common stocks since they are homogeneous financial assets.

Investors' considerations are in monetary terms (dollars in the U.S.). Investors purchase in dollars; investors receive benefits in dollars; and investors sell in dollars. There are no non-monetary benefits to common stock ownership. Common stock purchases and sales, particularly among easily-traded shares of publicly-held firms, are motivated purely by the monetary expected rate of return/risk relationships.

The prices of common shares continually change to reflect changes in the expected rate of return and/or the risk in an attempt to find equilibrium. The expected rate of return must be equilibrium compensation for the risk. We can envision these relationships:

(1) Expected Rate of Return (R) v. Risk

(2) Expected Rate of Return (R) = Expected to be Received
     $Benefits/Stock Price

If the $Benefits expected to be received from the corporation and/ or risk change, the equilibrium in relationship (1) is upset and must immediately be restored. The only immediate, restoring mechanism is a change in the common stock price.

For example, assume the expected $Benefits to be received (most likely, expected dividends) are suddenly lower. Also assume risk has not changed. The lower expected rate of return no longer sufficiently compensates for the unchanged risk. Current shareholders are motivated to sell and potential new buyers are no longer motivated to buy at the existing price. The common stock price must fall in relationship (2) so that equilibrium is restored in the following sequence. The expected $Benefits fall; the common stock price falls in turn causing the expected rate of return to again be at the prior level necessary to compensate for the unchanged risk. Equilibrium is restored to the expected rate of return/risk in relationship (1).

The converse sequence of event occurs if the expected $Benefits to be received increase. The expected rate of return/risk equilibrium in

Table 1.1
The Impact of Changes in Expected $Benefits and Risk on Stock Prices

	Expected $Benefits Change	Risk Change	Common Stock Price Change
1.	Increase	Unchanged	Increase
2.	Increase	Decrease	Increase Significantly
3.	Unchanged	Decrease	Increase
4.	Unchanged	Increase	Decrease
5.	Unchanged	Unchanged	Unchanged
6.	Decrease	Unchanged	Decrease
7.	Decrease	Increase	Decrease Significantly
8.	Increase	Increase	?
8a.	Increase greater than	Increase	Increase
8b.	Increase less than	Increase	Decrease
8c.	Increase equal to	Increase	Unchanged
9.	Decrease	Decrease	?
9a.	Decrease greater than	Decrease	Decrease
9b.	Decrease less than	Decrease	Increase
9c.	Decrease equal to	Decrease	Unchanged

relationship (1) is disrupted. The expected rate of return on the common stock price is higher and over-compensating for the unchanged risk. Current shareholders are no longer motivated to sell at the current common stock price. Potential new investors are motivated to purchase at a higher price. The common stock price must rise in relationship (2) so that the equilibrium in relationship (1) can be restored. Table 1.1 summarizes various combinations of changes in the expected $Benefits and/or risk that affect the common stock price.

The combinations of changes in the factors of relationships (1) and (2) cause the change in the common stock price. The numbered combinations from Table 1.1 have the following impacts on common stock prices:

1. An increase in expected $Benefits with unchanged risk implies an increased stock price. This combination of changes may occur only briefly as common stock prices fluctuate in response to economic activity (the economic/stock price cycle).

2. An increase in expected $Benefits accompanied by a decrease in risk significantly increases the common stock price more than in combination 1. Each change, by itself, tends to increase the common stock

price. The combination of both changes doubly affects the common stock price upward. This combination of changes occurs in the typical economic/stock price cycle. However, it does not last and is replaced by another combination of changes as the typical economic/stock price cycle progresses. The most likely location in the economic/stock price cycle for this combination of changes is shortly before the trough in economic activity.

3. An unchanged expected $Benefits accompanied by a decrease in risk implies an increased common stock price. This also occurs in the economic/stock price cycle, but typically lasts for a shorter time than do other combinations in Table 1.1.

4. An unchanged expected $Benefits accompanied by an increase in the risk implies a decrease in the common stock price. This combination of changes usually appears after the high in stock prices as economic activity heads toward its peak.

5. A combination of simultaneously unchanged expected $Benefits and risk is usually fleeting and fosters a stable stock price environment. Like the other combinations and their accompanying stock price environments, this combination is replaced as the factors in relationships (1) and (2) change and foster a different common stock price environment as the economic/stock price cycle progresses.

6. A decrease in expected $Benefits combined with unchanged risk fosters an environment of decreased common stock prices. This combination, like the others, is replaced as the economic/stock price cycle progresses.

7. A decrease in expected $Benefits accompanied by an increase in risk doubly, negatively affects common stock prices. This is the analogous but opposite direction of combination 2. The expected $Benefits and risk factors both foster decreased common stock prices. The combination of the two is, in effect, a double, negative impact on common stock prices. This combination usually occurs shortly after the peak in economic activity.

8. A combination of both expected $Benefit and risk simultaneously increasing has no clear directional impact on common stock prices. Each factor in the relationship pushes stock prices in the opposite direction. Investors can only tell the impact on common stock prices after they determine the relative change in each of the factors.

8a. If the increase in expected $Benefits is greater than the increase in risk, common stock prices increase. This combination fosters increasing common stock prices and tends to last the longest in the economic/stock price cycle.

8b. If the increase in expected $Benefits is less than the increase in risk, common stock prices decrease.

8c. If the expected $Benefits and the risk increase equally, common stock prices remain unchanged. This typically occurs fleetingly at the high in the stock price cycle.

9. A combination of expected $Benefits and risk simultaneously decreasing has no clear directional impact on common stock prices. Each factor in the relationship pushes common stock prices in the opposite direction. Investors can only tell the impact on common stock prices after they determine the relative change in each of the factors.

9a. If the decrease in expected $Benefits is greater than the decrease in risk, common stock prices fall. This combination occurs in economic recession. This combination is replaced as the economic/stock price cycle progresses.

9b. If the decrease in expected $Benefits is less than the decrease in risk, common stock prices increase. This combination occurs after a low in stock prices and before economic activity troughs. This combination passes as the economic/stock price cycle progresses.

9c. If expected $Benefits and risk decrease equally, common stock prices are unchanged. This typically occurs fleetingly at the low in common stock prices.

FACTORS, FLUCTUATIONS, FREQUENCY, ETC.?

Tantalizing, unanswered questions come to mind after absorbing Table 1.1:

Can the factors in relationships (1) and (2) of the combinations that cause common stock prices to increase or decrease be identified?

Can the causes that change these factors be identified?

Can these factors be measured?

Is there a conceptual interaction among the factors that explains common stock price fluctuations?

Do the combinations in Table 1.1 have different durations?

Which of the combinations in Table 1.1 occurs most frequently?

Do all the Table 1.1 combinations occur in every economic/ stock price cycle?

Do these combinations occur in any order or sequence over the economic/stock price cycle?

Are these changing combinations the forces behind fluctuations in common stock prices?

Are there implications for portfolio management and asset allocation in the various Table 1.1 combinations?

What types of asset allocation tactics can be used to maximize portfolio returns under the various combinations of Table 1.1?

Are there valuation implications for individual stocks?

Is there an explanation for sector rotation in the changing combinations of Table 1.1 as the economic/stock price cycle progresses?

Is the price/earnings multiple an effective shorthand for the valuation framework?

Is a company's stage of development associated with a particular Table 1.1 combination more than another?

Why ain't I rich?

The answer to all these questions, except "why ain't I rich?" is *Yes*. The following chapters provide more detailed answers.

By the way, the reason you "ain't rich," is that the answers to these questions depend on future events and changes. Foretelling the future with any accuracy is very, very hard. Investors may know what factors and relationships to look for after mastering Table 1.1 and reading this book, but forecasting them is another story. Better forecasters make better money.

SUMMARY

The relationship between expected rate of return and risk is intuitively obvious. The expected rate of return must appropriately compensate investors for the risk.

Individual investors can, at least subjectively, describe and rank each financial asset, including common stocks, by its expected rate of return/risk relationship. The top ranking is the highest expected rate of return for the risk or, conversely, the lowest risk for the expected rate of return.

Investors continually seek the highest-ranked common stocks in the expected rate of return/risk rankings. As changes occur in the rankings, investors switch their portfolio holdings, selling the lower-ranked for the higher-ranked shares. Each security is competing for the investor's dollar, causing investors to switch. This is easily done among publicly-traded common stocks because of their homogeneity and fungibility. Common stocks have only monetary rewards. There are no non-monetary considerations to distort the rankings. Investors distinguish among common stocks only by the monetary expected rate of return/risk relationship.

Combinations of the expected rate of return/risk relationship vary as the economic/stock price cycle progresses. Changes in either the expected rate of return and/or the risk interact to cause stock prices to increase or decrease. The factors within the relationship change as the economic/stock price cycle progresses, resulting in stock price fluctuations.

2

Causal Valuation Factors

What are the causal factors in the Table 1.1 combinations?

EXPECTED FUTURE $BENEFITS

The expected future dollar benefits ($Benefits) to be received by stockholders are dividends. They are the only benefit that can be transferred directly to the shareholder from the corporation. Dividends are paid out of earnings. So investors must look to earnings as the generator of expected future $Benefits. The natural consequence is that investors expend vast time and energy analyzing and forecasting earnings, particularly earnings per share. Corporate managements also spend energy and time on reported corporate earnings per share (see Appendix 2A).

Management must eventually transfer benefits from the corporation, a separate legal entity from stockholders, so the common share may have value. The share purchased is only a claim on *future*, expected dividends. If none is paid, the shareholder claim is worthless. Of course the shareholder may prefer that dividends be postponed while the corporation reinvests retained earnings to grow the expected dollar amount of future dividends.

KEYWORD "FUTURE"

The key word is future. The expected earnings and dividends generated as expected $Benefits to the shareholders must occur in the future. Past dividends belong to the past, even perhaps to a prior shareholder. A new shareholder cannot demand past dividends already received from a prior shareholder.

The claim on dividends accompanying any share is a future claim. A dollar received in the future is not worth as much as if it were received today. This is the concept of present value.

PRESENT VALUE

Why is a dollar received tomorrow not worth as much as a dollar received today? The wait is costly. At the very least, interest is lost. Investors pay a lower price for a claim on future dividends than the dollar amount of those expected dividends. The lower price is compensation for lost interest and the risk of waiting.

Investors also run the risk, particularly in common stocks, that adverse events might occur during the wait. The dividends actually received might be lower than the dividends expected when the common shares were bought. The common stock price will probably be lower if this occurs.

The future claim on dividends is infinite. Investors can own the shares forever. The shares are never intended to be redeemed. The expected life of the corporation is perpetuity. Publicly-traded companies rarely plan to remain in business for a limited number of years and then dissolve. Buying a share of common stock really means investors must forecast expected dividends infinitely into the future. If investors could perfectly foresee the future dividends, they could readily calculate the intrinsic value of the common shares at any particular discount rate. Such foresight is not possible.

DISCOUNTING

The required rate of return (r) that compensates shareholders for the lost interest and risk of the wait discounts future dividends to the present. The lost interest can be measured by the yield to maturity on a U.S. Treasury bond. The specific maturity varies among investors. However, long-term bond yields are probably the best proxy for lost interest since their maturities are closest to the assumed, infinite life of the common stock. Expected dividends beyond the long-term bond maturity have little impact on the present value of the common share at almost any historically-observed required rate of return (r) discount. There is no impact on the current common stock price because those dividends are expected so far in the future.

The required rate of return must be increased beyond the long-term U.S. Treasury Bond yield to include the risk that expected dividends might not be received. The required rate of return (r) is the discount rate used to calculate the present value of the expected dividends. The required rate of return reflects all risks associated with common share ownership. The expanded required rate of return for individual common stock is developed throughout subsequent chapters to include the major categories of risk that must be considered.

THE CURRENT COMMON STOCK PRICE

The current common stock price (P) is the present value of the market consensus, expected dividends discounted to the present value by the required rate of return.

This concept is captured in Equation (3):

$$P = \Sigma_{t=1, \infty} E_t(1 - \Lambda) / (1 + r)^t \tag{3}$$

where the symbols in Equation (3) stand for

P	= current share price of the common stock
$\Sigma_{t=1, \infty}$	= the sum of the future from now to infinity
E_t	= the expected future earnings in each future year t
Λ	= the percentage of the earnings (E) retained. Thus $1 - \Lambda$ is the payout rate. The numerator of the Equation (3) valuation framework is the expected dividend in each year t. Since Λ is assumed stable, it drops it from the equation to focus on earnings, the source of dividends.
r	= the required rate of return used to discount the future expected earnings, implying dividends, to the common share price (present value).

THE COMBINATIONS OF TABLE 1.1

The interacting factors of the Table 1.1 combinations are evident in the Equation (3) valuation framework. The numerator of the Equation (3) valuation framework is the expected $Benefits of Table 1.1, identified as expected future dividends. The denominator of the Equation (3) valuation framework is the risk of Table 1.1, identified as the required rate of return used as the discount rate in deriving the current common stock price (P) in the Equation (3) valuation framework.

An increase in the numerator of the Equation (3) valuation framework increases the common stock price. A decrease in the numerator of the Equation (3) valuation framework decreases the common stock price. An increase in the denominator of the Equation (3) valuation framework decreases the common stock price. A decrease in the denominator of the Equation (3) valuation framework increases the common stock price.

Counteracting changes in the numerator and denominator of the Equation (3) valuation framework offset each other. The relative rate of change in the numerator v. the denominator dictates whether the common stock price increases or decreases.

THE EXPECTED EARNINGS FACTOR (E)

Future earnings are an intuitively obvious factor in the valuation of common stock. Vast time and effort are spent forecasting earnings for the stock market as well as for specific corporations. Stock analysts and other experts continually examine the large number of variables that affect earnings. Their forecasts are widely and quickly disseminated through the most rapid and modern forms of telecommunications. These forecasts form the basis for the market consensus of future earnings as far as can be reasonably forecast. There is no need herein for us to explore how those forecasts, right or wrong, are derived or how they become the market consensus earnings forecast. The earnings consensus emerges and becomes E in the Equation (3) valuation framework.

Where can investors get consensus earnings forecasts? The answer, if the information is not already free, is to simply go to the Internet and subscribe.

THE RISK FACTOR (R)

The risk factor starts with the cornerstone of all investment alternatives, the lost interest rate on the long-term U.S. Treasury Bond.

It is default risk free. No other U.S. financial asset has that characteristic. Bondholders are always assured of getting their interest and redemption payments. The U.S. Government cannot run out of money. It prints more money in never-ending amounts, if needed. No corporation can legally do that.[1]

FUNGIBILITY AGAIN

Since all financial assets compete on an expected rate of return/risk basis, all financial assets, such as common stock, must have a higher expected rate of return than the long-term U.S. Treasury bond yield. All financial assets are risker than U.S. Treasury securities of the same maturity. A hierarchy of expected returns, rising in lockstep as risk rises, starts with the default-free U.S. Treasury yield as the lowest rung on the ladder. Every other financial asset is at a higher rung on the expected rate of return/risk ladder.

As the default-free U.S. Treasury bond yield (expected rate of return) climbs from the first rung, the expected rate of return on every other financial asset on that ladder must also climb. The U.S. Treasury bond yield increases while it remains default risk free. The required rate of return for all other financial assets, including common stock, must also climb. The holders and potential purchasers of those other financial assets can now buy default-risk-free U.S. Treasury securities with a higher yield. Investors in other securities are no longer appropriately compensated for risk (see relationship 2) relative to this higher default-free rate of return from the U.S. Treasury bond. Investors sell or no longer potentially buy common stocks or other financial assets at their prevailing prices. Common stock prices must drop to raise the expected rate of return to compete with the fungible U.S. Treasury security higher yield. The reverse process occurs when U.S. Treasury bond yields fall.

Fungibility restores equilibrium to the expected rate of return/risk rankings. In terms of the Equation (3) valuation framework, the required rate of return has increased in response to the increased U.S. Treasury bond yield. The discount rate in the denominator must also increase. The common stock price must decrease, provided expected earnings in the numerator remain unchanged. Conversely, fungibility also restores equilibrium at higher prices for common stocks and other financial assets when U.S. Treasury bond yields decrease.

What causes the identified earnings (E) and risk (R) factors to change?

CHANGING EARNINGS (E)

Earnings change with the economic cycle. Corporate earnings increase during economic expansion and decline or slow in economic contraction. Changes in expected earnings (E) in the numerator of the Equation (3) valuation framework affect common stock prices. As corporate earnings rise, common stock prices rise. As corporate earnings fall, common stock prices fall.

The speed of change in corporate earnings over the economic cycle also affects common stock prices. Acceleration and deceleration in the rate of change in corporate earnings affect common stock prices. This is reflected in the numerator of the Equation (3) valuation framework, assuming unchanged risk in the denominator:

More rapid increase in expected earnings (E) causes more upward pressure on common stock prices.

Less rapid increase in expected earnings causes less upward pressure on common stock prices.

More rapid decrease in expected earnings causes more downward pressure on common stock prices.

Less rapid decrease in expected earnings causes less downward pressure on common stock prices.

The sensitivity of specific corporate earnings varies in response to the economic cycle. The earnings of a few companies are counter-cyclical. Heightened earnings sensitivity to the economic cycle increases the associated risk.

Predicting future earnings is harder for more cyclical-sensitive corporations, and a shortfall or surpassing of their consensus earnings forecasts is more likely. When surprise differences from the consensus earnings forecast occur, expected earnings (E) in the Equation (3) valuation framework must be adjusted. The stock price must change to a lower or higher equilibrium price for the risk in the denominator of the Equation (3) valuation framework.

More specific impacts on earnings for individual industries or companies beyond the general economic cycle are often observed. The earnings for each firm are captured in the numerator of the Equation (3) valuation framework. A change in a specific company's expected earnings also changes its common stock price. The earnings impact for specific corporate common stock prices is explored in later chapters.

CHANGING RISK (R)—THE NOMINAL INTEREST RATE

The observed long-term U.S. Treasury bond interest rate is a nominal interest rate. It is also a major part of the risk factors in the Equation (3) valuation framework denominator. As already noted, the long-term U.S. Treasury bond interest rate is the lowest, and the cornerstone expected rate of return against which the expected rate of return on every common stock and other assets is compared. As it fluctuates, so do all other expected rates of return, including the denominator in the Equation (3) valuation framework for common stock prices.

Changes in the nominal interest rate respond to changes in the supply and demand for money and inflation expectations. Like any other commodity, money has a price, known as the interest rate. As the demand for money increases, there is upward pressure on interest rates and vice versa. As the supply of money decreases, there is upward pressure on interest rates and vice versa. The observed, nominal interest rate is the equilibrating price for the supply and demand of money.

The Federal Reserve System (Fed) controls, to a great extent, the money supply. The Fed changes the money supply in an attempt to meet its goals of full employment, price stability, economic growth, and balance of payments equilibrium. In the process, common stock prices are affected.

The Fed increases or decreases the money supply in response to the economic cycle and, by unavoidable consequence, affects common stock prices. When economic activity is slow or depressed, usually accompanied by high unemployment and little or no economic growth, the Fed increases the money supply, putting downward pressure on interest rates. The consequence is upward pressure on common stock prices since the risk factor in the denominator of the Equation (3) valuation framework is decreased.

When economic activity is rising or booming, usually accompanied by moderate or rapid inflation, respectively, the Fed decreases the money supply, putting upward pressure on interest rates. The consequence is downward pressure on stock prices since the denominator in the Equation (3) valuation framework is increased.

Investors must remain carefully attuned to the economic environment that motivates the Fed. Domestic concerns of full employment, economic growth, and price stability motivate the Fed to money supply and interest rate action.

International considerations occasionally move the Fed. Prolonged attempts by other nations to increase their exports to the U.S. to solve their own domestic recessions could pose an economic threat that must be adroitly handled by the Fed. Investors have a difficult task predicting Fed actions since the Fed objectives may be conflicting. For example, spurring economic growth requires lower interest rates that may also boost unwanted inflation expectations. Achieving appropriate balance is a difficult art.

THE COMPONENTS OF THE NOMINAL INTEREST RATE

The observed nominal interest rate partly reflects the interest rate paid purely for the use of money. This is the real interest rate. Another part of the nominal interest rate on the long-term U.S. Treasury bond compensates investors for lost purchasing power caused by inflation. This is the purchasing power risk premium. The combination of the two is

$$r = i + p$$

where

r   = the nominal interest rate

i   = compensation for the use of money only (the real interest rate)

p   = purchasing power risk premium in addition to i

The nominal interest rate (r) rises and falls as each of its components rises or falls.

THE REAL INTEREST RATE (i)

The nominal interest rate component strictly related to compensation for the use of money, without regard to the risk of inflation, is the real interest rate (i). That rate is determined by the supply and demand for money. The Fed, as already noted, is a major factor in the supply of money but not the only one. Commercial banks, through which the Fed operates, and other financial institutions must be willing to loan the money. The mechanism breaks down if lenders do not make the money supplied to them available to borrowers.

Individuals must save, providing supply to the market place. Foreign investors must invest in the U.S. markets, especially if U.S. savers are not supplying enough savings to meet the entire domestic demand for money.

The Fed is the biggest supplier of money and can, to a significant degree, control the short-term interest rate. Every Fed move is scrutinized. Changes in the supply and/or the demand for money cause changes in the real interest rate. Downward or upward Fed interest rate pressures affect the denominator in the Equation (3) valuation framework and inversely affect common stock prices.

The demand for money mostly reflects economic activity and the government budget surplus or deficit. As economic activity increases, the demand for money increases. Business and consumer demand rises for the purchase of homes, durable and non-durable goods, and for new plant and equipment. This does not occur uniformly throughout the economic/stock price cycle and has implications for portfolio sector rotation and individual common stock valuation.

The demand for money by the U.S. government has been likened to the eight hundred-pound gorilla. Whatever amount of money it wants, it gets, regardless of the interest rate it must pay. If the U.S. Treasury wants more money, it simply borrows. The effect may be an increased U.S. Treasury bond yield, the cornerstone of all yields and required rates of return. As the U.S. Treasury bond yield increases, all other interest rates and the denominator in the Equation (3) valuation framework increase, putting downward pressure on common stock prices. Federal government budget surpluses have the opposite effect.

PURCHASING POWER RISK PREMIUM (p)

During the time investors have their money invested in the bond or other financial assets and not available to purchase goods and services, inflation may erode purchasing power. Investors must incorporate the expected inflation rate into the required yield to maturity. As the rate of inflation expected over the life of the bond increases, interest rates must rise by the same amount. The nominal interest rate observed and used in the denominator of the Equation (3) valuation framework consists of a real interest rate component and a purchasing risk premium component.

Changes in the purchasing power risk premium reflect the inflation rate and emanate from the same causes and economic circumstances. The most obvious inflation scenario is too much demand for available goods and services, forcing up prices. This is best described as the classic demand/pull inflation and is typically observed around the peak in economic activity. The consequence of this or any other type of inflation is higher prices and higher interest rates. This is reflected as an increase in the denominator of the Equation (3) valuation framework, putting downward pressure on common stock prices.

Cost/push inflation is the other, most typical type of inflation over the last several decades. Cost/push inflation generally arises when the costs of production, such as labor or raw materials, rise. Unable to sustain satisfactory profit margins because of rising costs, companies increase prices. The result is inflation. The consequences are the same as in all other types of inflation. Interest rates rise. The denominator in the Equation (3) valuation framework also rises. Stock prices fall for the expected earnings.

THE INTERACTION OF EARNINGS (E) AND RISK (R)

Like all factors that affect stock prices, the interaction between expected earnings and risk are captured in the Equation (3) valuation framework. A change in the earnings (E) numerator of the Equation (3) valuation framework directly affects the common stock price. A change in the risk denominator of the Equation (3) valuation framework inversely affects the common stock price. A prevailing common stock price (P) reflects the present value from now to infinity of its consensus expected earnings (E) discounted at the prevailing risk (R) required rate of return. An individual investor's valuation may or may not agree with the current common stock price (P), depending on the investor's expected earnings and perceived risk.

Can these identified factors and their causes be measured?

MEASURES OF EARNINGS (E) AND RISK (R)

The identified factors of earnings and interest rate risk may be historically tracked and measured. Forecasting these factors is and will always be an imperfect art. Past performance is not an indication of future performance. Investors must, however, use the past to be sensitive to the future in which general, as well as specific, common stock prices will be determined.

EARNINGS MEASURES (E)

Past earnings are readily available from numerous sources with considerable but not perfect accuracy, as there are occasional historical revisions. Future earnings forecasts are also readily available from numerous sources with much less accuracy and frequent revisions. These revisions change the numerator in the Equation (3) valuation framework and contribute to common stock price changes.

The more accurate earnings forecasters profit from the changes in earnings forecasts as the stock market must adjust the common stock price to agree with their more accurate forecasts. These changes create profit opportunities for some and losses for others. Unfortunately no one is always right or wrong in earnings forecasts. The earnings forecasts of those who are right half the time and wrong half the time are potentially the most difficult and costly for investors to use in their valuations. The forecasts of those who are always right or wrong are valuable. Investors profit by following the former and doing exactly the opposite of the latter.

RISK MEASURES (R)

The two basic categories of risk to this point are the real interest rate and the purchasing power risk premium (inflation). Changes in either one of these components of the nominal interest rate cause common stock prices to change in the opposite direction as reflected in the Equation (3) valuation framework.

SUPPLY/DEMAND FOR MONEY

A considerable number of statistics track the supply and demand for money. These range from very direct measures of money supply, such as M1, M2, and M3, money market mutual fund assets, and the monetary base to more indirect indications, such as the excess held by banks above required reserves (free reserves) and total bank loans. A summary and definitions of many of these measures appear in Appendix 2B.

Real interest rates are usually lower and liquidity higher when the money supply increases at relatively rapid rates. The Fed often judges an appropriate range for the rate of growth in these measures, implying a tightening or loosening bent to monetary policy. The degree of implementation can swerve between public pronouncements of such ranges, depending on the economic/stock price cycle.

Fed policy implementation depends on the financial institutions conduit through which its policy actions reach the money and bond markets. Occasionally banks do not loosen or restrict the supply of money as intended by Fed actions. Banks may not lend the money supplied by the Fed but instead increase reserves. The availability of credit does not increase. Fed efforts to lower interest rates or keep them from not increasing may be thwarted. The Fed-induced increased money supply never reaches the markets. Existing demand is not satisfied. Interest rates rise. Of course the reverse occurs if the Fed implements tightening, but banks and other financial institutions reduce their reserves and continue to lend.

Symptomatic measures of the degree to which the bank conduit reflects Fed policy include bank-free reserves, total and particular classifications of bank loans, the proportion of bank investment in securities relative to loans, the yield spread between U.S. Treasury securities and bonds of lesser quality. These measures are frequently reported and readily available through numerous media.

A careful interpretation of these and other measures reveals the degree of available credit. In economic expansion, declining loan activity, higher free reserves, and an increasing proportion of security investment relative to loans indicate a slowing supply of money reaching the market. Interest rates usually respond by rising. A widening yield spread (the difference between yields on bonds of the same ma-turity but of different quality) indicates that lenders perceive increased risk. Less money is available to the riskier borrowers. Interest rates on high-quality bonds, such as U.S. Treasuries, decrease while inter-est rates on lower-quality bonds increase. This is another sign that a Fed loosening policy is not reaching the market. An opposite profile of these measures indicates decreasing interest rates.

INFLATION

The most obvious measures of inflation are price indexes. Among the more commonly followed of these are the Producer Price Index, the Consumer Price Index, and the gross domestic price deflator. The more volatile components, such as crude oil and agricultural prices, are often removed to reflect the core inflation rate. These inflation measures may be associated with any type of inflation, such as de-mand/pull or cost/push.

Demand/Pull Inflation

Demand/pull inflation is classically described as "too much money chasing too few goods." Excessive money-supply growth, usually cre-ated by the Fed in an effort to stimulate the economy, has historically fostered demand/pull inflation several months after the injection of excessive money supply. A counterbalancing impact on common stock prices usually occurs between the direct effect of the change in the money supply and the accompanying expectations of the subsequent, inflationary impact on interest rates.

The immediate impact of an increase in the money supply on the prevailing money demand reduces interest rates and creates liquidity. This typically fosters higher common stock prices because the de-nominator in the Equation (3) valuation framework falls. On the other hand, investors worry that the high, possibly excessive, rate of growth in the money supply will eventually push demand beyond the supply of goods and services, forcing up prices. This worry leads to higher inflation expectations and interest rates and fosters lower stock prices as the denominator in the Equation (3) valuation framework rises.

Investor reaction depends on the current location in the economic/stock price cycle. A rapidly increasing injection of money supply when the economy is approaching or at the trough in economic activity leads to lower interest rates and higher stock prices. That same rapidly increasing injection of money supply when approaching or at the peak in economic activity usually leads to heightened inflation expectations, higher interest rates and lower stock prices as reflected in the Equation (3) valuation framework.

Cost/Push Inflation

When inflation rises more from the push of costs, investors often look at measures in the underlying areas of price pressure. These areas are labor costs, raw materials costs, and foreign exchange rates. Most cost pressure has historically risen from increased labor costs and consequent profit-margin squeezes. Corporations respond by increasing prices to maintain profits and profit growth, if the costs cannot be offset by increased productivity and price competition permits.

Raw materials costs are another area of cost pressure. The Commodity Research Bureau, Goldman Sachs, and National Association of Purchasing Management Survey indexes of inflation are a few of the more widely disseminated measures. Several of these indexes use future prices and are more forward-looking. Changes in future prices often change investors' inflation expectations.

Foreign exchange rates with major trading partners are another, usually less contributing pressure in cost/push inflation. As the price of imported goods is forced up by a declining U.S. dollar, possibly with accompanying price increases from competing, domestically-produced goods, inflation rises. Conversely lower prices on imported goods from a rising U.S. dollar may exert downward price pressures and lower U.S. inflation.

Cost/push inflation pressures are offset by increased productivity that allows producers to maintain profits and profit margins without raising prices. Competitive price pressure may prohibit price increases even if productivity does not increase. Then expected earnings fall and common stock prices drop.

Yield Curve Measures

The yield curve on U.S. Treasury securities sometimes offers insights into expected inflation. The traditional upward-sloping yield curve, with lower short-term and higher long-term interest rates, reflects investor expectations that the economy will continue to expand and interest rates will rise. The purchasing power risk premium is also embedded in the yield curve. Investor compensation for expected inflation forces longer-term yields to be higher. This reflects purchasing power lost while investors hold the bond in their portfolios.

The most explicit indication of the embodied purchasing power risk premium in the interest rate is the difference between the inflation-indexed U.S. Treasury bond yield and the traditional (not inflation-indexed) bond yield of the same maturity. The only difference in the yields should be investors' expected purchasing power risk. This measure allows investors to distinguish between the real interest rate caused by the supply/demand for money and the purchasing power risk premium for specific maturities.

The U.S. Treasury yield curve has configurations other than upward sloping (see Appendix 3A). A downward-sloping configuration typically implies investor expectations of future, lower interest rates. This shape is usually a precursor of recession. Current demand for a limited supply of money, which may have intentionally been restricted by the Fed to fight inflation at or near the peak in economic activity, exceeds supply. A scramble for money, known as a credit crunch, may occur. Interest rates spike. Stock prices decline as the denominator in the Equation (3) valuation framework also spikes. Every major interest rate spike has been associated with a major common stock price decline. The interest rate spike is usually temporary. As the economy unwinds into recession, the credit crunch turns into a normal recession pattern of lower money demand, higher Fed-induced money supply, and lower interest rates.

Investors sometimes use a rule-of-thumb approximation to estimate the inflation-adjusted interest rate. Using the historical U.S. average 3.0% to 3.5% real interest rate (i), investors simply add their expected inflation rate (p) and derive an expected nominal interest rate (i + p).

SUMMARY

The factors in the combinations of Table 1.1 and the Equation (3) valuation framework that underlie common stock prices are future earnings and the risk of realizing them. Changes in these factors cause common stock prices to change.

The causes for changes in expected earnings and the associated risk are numerous and varied. However, general patterns have emerged.

Expected earnings, on average, fluctuate with the economic cycle. Earnings are anticipated to rise in expansion and fall in recession for most companies. The consensus expected earnings are the numerator of the Equation (3) valuation framework.

The causes of changes in risk start with the yield available on fungible securities. The U.S. Treasury bond yield is the cornerstone of fungibility. That yield is default risk free. Any security with risk of defaulting on its expected benefits must afford investors a higher yield. Since future earnings on common stocks can and do default on expected earnings, the required rate of return (yield) on common stock is higher.

As U.S. Treasury bond yields fluctuate so must the yields on all other securities, including common stocks. The U.S. Treasury bond yield fluctuates with changes in the real interest rate and the purchasing power risk premium. The former responds to the supply and demand for money. The latter responds to inflation expectations.

Investors try to measure the underlying causes for changes in real interest rates and inflation. Measures include various price indexes, such as the Producer and Consumer Price Indexes. More forward-looking measures include commodity future prices and yield curve and yield spread implications.

NOTE

1. Some corporations have tried to issue never-ending amounts of highly valued shares in place of currency. Of course, the continuous issuance eventually depraves the stock price. Governments have also tried to issue never-ending amounts of currency. They, too, ultimately fail; such as Germany after World War I.

Appendix 2A

Reported Earnings Considerations

ACCRUAL VS. CASH ACCOUNTING

Accrual accounting employs the principle of matching revenues with expenses concurrently. Any delays between the sale (expenditure) and the associated collection (payment) of cash are reflected in intermediate (accrual) accounts, such as accounts receivable. In contrast, cash accounting recognizes all sales and other transactions only when the associated cash is paid or received. Virtually all public companies use the accrual method.

A company may report a profit under accrual accounting methods while technically insolvent or bankrupt because it has no cash to pay its bills. Sales and accounts receivable may grow, accounts payable must be paid, but no cash flows in until the accounts receivable are collected. The mistiming between the cash inflows and the cash outflows may cause insolvency. The very exaggerated example below illustrates this.

Assume:
Starting cash is $10 million
All costs are 80% of sales
Accounts receivable are collected every 30 days (1 period later)
Accounts payable are paid in the same period as sales

The company would report a profit on its income statement:

ABC, Inc. Income Statement ($millions)

Period	0	1	2	3
Sales		10	20	30
Costs		8	16	24
Profit		2	4	6

However, the balance sheet reveals insolvency:

ABC, Inc. Balance Sheet ($millions)

Period	0	1	2	3
Cash	10	2	−4	−8
Accounts Rec.		10	20	30

ABC, Inc. has no money to pay its bills by the end of period two despite reporting profits on rapidly growing sales. The accounts receivable necessary to support the rapid sales growth has depleted the firm's cash. The accrual accounting method has correctly recognized the timing match between sales and accounts receivable but failed to recognize the delay between sales and the cash collection of the associated accounts receivable. The firm has profitably grown itself into insolvency. Investors must pay careful attention to the statement of cash flows that records the timing of the cash inflows and cash outflows.

Reliance on reported earnings per share may overlook important considerations in the "quality" of those earnings. Common stock valuation is based on fundamental recurring earnings capacity. In other words, "quality earnings" that truly reflect company operations.

ACCOUNTS RECEIVABLE

Accounts receivable are accruals that may not be collected. Bad debt charges and provisions are usually a management judgment, subject to overestimation or underestimation and mistiming. The result may be distorted reported earnings per share that, in turn, may distort the common stock valuation.

INVENTORY

The chosen method of reporting inventory may also distort reported earnings. The first-in-first-out (FIFO) method overstates reported earnings during inflation. The goods produced at the earlier, low cost are the first sold at the higher, inflated price. The reported profit may be nonrecurring and disappear once the lower-cost produced inventory is sold. Financial statements provided to investors do not reveal how much of reported inventory is lower cost.

The last-in-first-out (LIFO) method of reporting inventory understates reported profits during inflation. Companies can switch inventory reporting methods, although sometimes IRS consent is required.

SALES

Sales may not fall within a particular accounting period. A sale may fall outside the selected calendar-ending date for a quarter or year-end financial statement. Reported earnings may differ from expected earnings as a result. Seasonal sales also affect reported earnings. Investors should be very cautious in extrapolating quarterly earnings to estimated annual earnings.

Different sales approaches affect the timing of expected revenues and earnings. The timing of expected earnings for a company that leases will differ from that of an identical company selling the same product. Common stock valuations based on the discounted present valuation framework are affected.

RESEARCH AND DEVELOPMENT

Research and development costs are usually expensed as incurred. A development-stage product can generate no revenues while incurring substantial costs, resulting in lower reported earnings. Then after development is complete, revenues are generated while costs recede, resulting in higher reported earnings. The juxtaposition of the reported losses and reported profits is quick and possibly large. Investors must recognize how and when this occurs under accounting conventions.

NON-RECURRING EARNINGS, GAINS, AND LOSSES

Common stock valuation must be based on fundamental, recurring earnings. Nonrecurring earnings, gains, or losses (unless they are fatally large) should be excluded. Nonrecurring items arise from numerous events. Investors must be alert and cognizant.

DEFERRED INCOMES TAXES

Deferred income taxes arise when accelerated depreciation is used. They may never be paid as long as the company asset base grows. Deferred taxes often lead to several sets of accounting books. One set for the taxing authorities and one set for stockholders. Additional sets may exist for regulators, foreign-taxing authorities, and others. This is legal.

MINORITY AND UNCONSOLIDATED INTERESTS

A company may incorporate its proportional interest in the profits of another partially-owned company in which it has invested but may not be able to use the other firm's generated cash. Companies may not report (consolidate) the operations of affiliated companies in their own financial statements despite being financially responsible. Investors must be particularly aware of any unconsolidated losses.

CAPITALIZING VS. EXPENSING

The judgment to capitalize rather than expense a cost or cash outlay changes reported and expected earnings. A practice in the oil exploration industry to capitalize dry holes as assets and then gradually write them off may distort the currently reported earnings, especially in comparison to other oil companies that expense dry holes.

HISTORICAL COST

Reported assets may be carried on the books at a cost that does not reflect current value. The current value may be higher or lower.

OFF-BALANCE SHEET FINANCING

Operating leases are examples of off-balance sheet financing. The operating lease, while real and binding, is not reflected directly in the reported financial statements. It is usually reported in the accompanying footnotes. Investors must be attuned and adjust where necessary.

GOODWILL AND INTANGIBLES

Goodwill and intangibles are nonphysical assets that may or may not have value despite being reported on the books. Conversely, valuable intangible assets may not be reported. Human capital, like highly valuable employees, and brand names are examples.

CONTINGENCIES

Contingent liabilities, such as pending lawsuits and possible adverse judgments, may be financially significant. These contingencies are reported only in the footnotes that accompany the reported financial statements and are rarely quantified.

Appendix 2B

Definitions

M1: The sum of currency held outside the vaults of depository institutions, Federal Reserve Banks, and the U.S. Treasury; travelers checks; and demand and other checkable deposits issued by financial institutions, except demand deposits due to the Treasury and depository institutions, minus cash items in process of collection and Federal Reserve float.

M2: M1 plus: savings and small denomination (less than $100,000) time deposits issued by financial institutions; and shares in retail money market mutual funds (funds with initial investments of less than $50,000), net of retirement accounts.

M3: M2 plus: large denomination ($100,000 or more) time deposits; repurchase agreements issued by depository institutions; Eurodollar deposits, specifically, dollar-denominated deposits due to nonbank U.S. addresses held at foreign offices of U.S. banks worldwide and all banking offices in Canada and the United Kingdom; and institutional money market mutual funds (funds with initial investments of $50,000 or more).

L: M3 plus: U.S. savings bonds, short-term Treasury securities, commercial paper, and bankers acceptances held by households and by firms other than depository institutions and money market mutual funds.

Bank Credit: all loans, leases and securities held by commercial banks.

Domestic Nonfinancial Debt: total credit market liabilities of the U.S. Treasury, federally sponsored agencies, state and local governments, households, and firms except depository institutions and money market mutual funds.

Note: The above six series are constructed and published by the Board of Governors of the Federal Reserve System, Washington, D.C. For details, see *Federal Reserve Bulletin*, tables 1.21 and 1.26.

MZM: M2 minus small denomination time deposits, plus institutional money market mutual funds. The label MZM was coined by William Poole (1991) for this aggregate, proposed earlier by Motley (1988). On pages four and six, MZM prior to January 1984 is not shown due to distortions caused by regulatory changes, including the introduction of liquid deposit account; not subject to binding interest rate ceilings.

Adjusted Monetary Base: the sum of currency in circulation outside Federal Reserve Banks and the U.S. Treasury, deposits of depository financial institutions at Federal Reserve Banks, and an adjustment for the effects of changes in statutory reserve requirements on the quantity of base money held by depositories. This series is a spliced chain index; see Anderson and Rasche (1996a, b).

Adjusted Reserves: the sum of vault cash and Federal Reserve Bank deposits held by depository institutions, and an adjustment for the effects of changes in statutory reserve requirements on the quantity of base money held by depositories. This series, a spliced chain index, is numerically larger than the Board of Governors' measure which excludes vault cash not used to satisfy statutory reserve requirements and Federal Reserve Bank deposits used to satisfy required clearing balance

contracts; see Anderson and Rasche (1996a) and http://www.stls.frb.
org/research/newbase.html.

Monetary Services Index: an index which measures the flow of monetary services received by households and firms from their holdings of liquid assets; see Anderson, Jones and Nesmith (1997). Indexes are shown for the assets included in M2 and L; additional data are available at http://www.stls.frb.org/research/msi/index.html.

Note: The above four series are constructed and published by the Research Division of the Federal Reserve Bank of St. Louis, St. Louis MO.

Source: *Monetary Trends*, Federal Reserve Bank of St. Louis, February 1999

3

Causal Valuation Factors Interaction

Is there a conceptual interaction among the identified causal factors that explains common stock price fluctuations?

RELATIVE RATES OF CHANGE

The identified causal factors of expected earnings and risk (identified as interest rates to this point) interact in the Equation (3) valuation framework to explain common stock price fluctuations. The significant concept for investors is the relative rates of change in each causal factor. The rate of change in expected earnings of the numerator may be smaller or larger than the rate of change in interest rates in the denominator of the Equation (3) valuation framework. The causal factor with the larger rate of change dominates and dictates the direction of common stock prices.

The rate of change may be large even for a small, absolute change, particularly for interest rates. Interest rates tend to fluctuate around a long-term average. Over time, U.S. interest rates, as measured by the long-term U.S. Treasury bond yield, average between 5% and 10% with occasional higher spikes or lower dips. Even a relatively small, absolute interest rate change calculated on a small base figure is a relatively large rate of change. For example a 1% increase in interest rates from 4% to 5% is a 25% rate of change in interest rates. This would represent significant downward pressure on common stock prices within the Equation (3) valuation framework. An equally large upward rate of change in expected earnings is required to offset the negative rate of change impact from the increase in interest rates.

Fluctuations in interest rates are sharper and shorter than fluctuations in expected earnings. Interest rates use a smaller base in the rate of change calculation. The combined effect of these two tendencies causes the rate of change in interest rates to dominate common stock price changes in short spurts. The pronounced spikes and dips do not last long, interest rates return to "normal" averages, and common stock prices are affected accordingly.

Expected total corporate earnings usually experience longer sustained growth following the pattern that economic expansions usually last longer than economic contractions. Fluctuations in expected total corporate earnings are less pronounced than those in interest rates. The base from which the rate of change in expected total earnings is calculated is larger than that used for interest rates. Further, the speed at which change in total expected earnings occurs is slower. For example a relatively large $10 billion increase in total expected earnings from $200 billion to $210 billion is a relatively small 5% rate of change. That rate of change could be easily overshadowed by a relatively small, absolute change in interest rates.

The interaction between the relative rates of change in interest rates and expected earnings over the economic/stock price cycle underlies the typical common stock price cycles, illustrated in Figure 3.1.

STAGE I

Starting at slightly before the trough (T) in economic activity, denoted in Stage I of Figure 3.1, economic activity is slack, the demand for money is low, and the supply of money is relatively high. Interest rates are low and probably still falling, putting upward pressure on common stock prices through the denominator of the Equation (3) valuation framework. Common stock prices are low, however, because the recession has depressed earnings more rapidly than interest rates have fallen until this point. When the rate of decrease in expected earnings equals the rate of decrease in interest rates, common stock prices reach their low, denoted as L in Figure 3.1. When the rate of decrease in expected earnings becomes less than the rate of

Figure 3.1
Economics/Stock Price Cycle

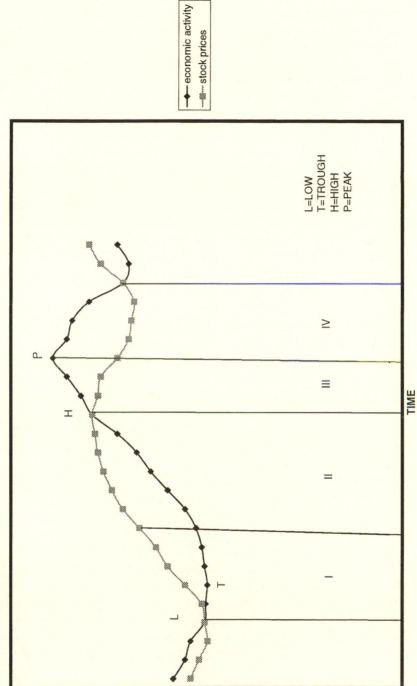

L=LOW
T=TROUGH
H=HIGH
P=PEAK

TIME

economic activity
stock prices

decrease in interest rates, stock prices rise. This occurs before the trough in economic activity, denoted as T in Figure 3.1.

As investors look beyond the valley in expected earnings to the recovery, expected earnings start to increase, putting upward pressure on common stock prices through an increase in the numerator of the Equation (3) valuation framework. Interest rates are probably still falling since the economy continues to decline, albeit at a slower rate as it moves toward the recession trough. The Fed may still be fighting the recession with money supply growth and lower interest rates. This is combination 2 from Table 1.1, and is one of the most pronounced upward (bullish) stages in common stock prices in the economic/stock price cycle.

The rate of increase in expected earnings is greatest at this point in the economic/stock price cycle. Companies have been slimming down through the recession. They are at their most efficient operating position. Any envisioned increase in sales will spur expected corporate earnings significantly since contribution margins will be the highest at these leanest operating positions.

The envisioned acceleration in expected earnings is further spurred by the release of pent-up consumer demand that built throughout the preceding recession. The consumer has spent less and saved more during the preceding economic decline for any number of logical, behavioral reasons, including the fear of job loss, lower confidence, smaller pay raises, etc. Investors anticipate that the envisioned economic recovery will open consumer purse strings. Resurgent consumer demand meets the efficient corporate ability to supply that demand at high profit margins. Expected earnings in the numerator of the Equation (3) valuation framework increase significantly. Common stock prices rise significantly.

This most rapid rise in common stock prices, starting from their cycle low before the trough in the economy, is the early part of Stage I in Figure 3.1. Stage I reflects a rapid rate of increase in expected earnings and a continuing, perhaps slowing rate of decrease (but a decrease nonetheless) in interest rates, which is combination 2 from Table 1.1. This most favorable of combinations for rising stock prices from Table 1.1 is usually relatively short. Many investors miss this quick, upward turn in common stock prices because their perspectives remain anchored in the tail end of the most recent prior stage that, in this case, was recession. The economic part of the economic/stock price cycle remains in recession. The common stock price part of that cycle is rising in anticipation of economic and earnings recovery. Common stock prices continue to rise throughout Stage I. Expected earnings are increasing relatively rapidly. Interest rates are increasing mildly.

STAGE II

Stage II in the economic/stock price cycle of Figure 3.1 has a different combination of rates of change for earnings and interest rates (risk). The economic expansion, started in Stage I, accelerates. The demand for money increases. The Fed may slightly slow the supply of money. Interest rates begin to rise.

The rate of growth in expected earnings may be slower, but expected earnings still grow. The costs of production start to rise marginally. Corporate efficiency slackens slightly. The net effect is that earnings are still rising but at a slower rate.

From the perspective of the Equation (3) valuation framework, expected earnings in the numerator still increase at a faster rate than the interest rate risk in the denominator. Common stock prices continue to rise, but at a slower rate of increase than in Stage I. The early Stage I double-positive effect on stock prices from the combination of increasing expected earnings *and* decreasing interest rates has gone. Returns to common stocks retreat from the relatively high rates experienced during Stage I, but remain positive throughout Stage II, one of the longest stages in the economic/stock price cycle.

The progression in the rates of change in expected earnings and in interest rates continues throughout Stage II. The expected earnings in the numerator of the Equation (3) valuation framework continue to increase but at a decreasing rate. At the beginning of Stage II the biggest spurt in pent-up demand for consumer durables, such as cars and housing, fueled by the stable low to declining interest rates has passed. A considerable portion of that pent-up demand has been satisfied. Increased economic activity slightly lifts interest rates. Marginal borrowers are eliminated. The maximum economies of scale experienced by goods and service producers when those firms were leanest, during Stage I, begin to lessen. This decrease may be slight at the beginning of Stage II. However, earnings efficiency will cumulatively diminish throughout Stage II as the most trained, ex-

perienced, and efficient workers are paid overtime and then supple-
mented with less trained, less experienced, and less efficient workers
to meet growing product and services demand.

Contribution profit margins shrink. Earnings continue to grow but
at a decreasing rate throughout Stage II. The rate of increase slows
as Stage II progresses. The fastest rate of increase in expected earnings in Stage II occurs at the beginning and then decelerates throughout Stage II and beyond to the peak in economic activity.

A slowing in the rate of growth in expected earnings occurs
throughout Stage II. Expected earnings in the Equation (3) valuation
framework numerator rise more slowly. Simultaneously, increasing
interest rates in the denominator of the Equation (3) valuation framework are partially offsetting. Common stock prices continue to rise
but not as rapidly as in Stage I. Combination 8a of Table 1.1 is
observed.

The relative rates of increase in expected earnings and interest rates
of Combination 8a of Table 1.1 are most significant. The expected
earnings are increasing at a slower rate of increase than in Stage I.
However, that increase remains larger than the rate of increase in
interest rates. These are offsetting impacts on common stock prices.
The positively impacting rate of increase in the expected earnings
offsets the negatively impacting rate of increase in interest rates. In
other words the numerator is rising faster than the denominator of
the Equation (3) valuation framework. Common stock prices rise
throughout Stage II.

Common stock prices still rise but more slowly than in Stage I,
when there was no or little offset between the rates of increase in
expected earnings and interest rates. In early Stage I, expected earnings were rising at an increasing rate and interest rates were stable to
falling. In later Stage I, expected earnings still rose relatively rapidly
while interest rates rose relatively slightly. Both the numerator and
the denominator of the Equation (3) valuation framework were putting upward pressure on common stock prices in early Stage I and
only slightly offsetting pressure on common stock prices in later Stage
I. In contrast the relative rates of change in expected earnings and
interest rates exert greater offsetting pressures on common stock
prices in Stage II.

A decelerating rate of growth in the expected earnings emerges as
Stage II progresses. Productivity and efficiency slacken. The core production personnel are taxed to their full effort. Firms incur overtime

costs to meet heightened demand for their goods and services. Middle management expands as senior managers, who took on middle-management responsibility during the recession and profit squeeze, can no longer physically meet the time demands of the required effort or choose not to do so. A second, less experienced, and less well-trained production shift is hired to meet increasing demand. The second shift incurs an expensive learning curve and takes time to reach the efficiency of the core staff. The associated added costs pinch profit margins. The rate of increase in expected earnings decreases.

The decrease in the rate of expected earnings growth accelerates as Stage II progresses. Labor and raw materials costs rise. Wages, salaries, and benefits rise as unemployment decreases. The growing demand for raw materials causes upward price pressures for those materials. Productivity falls under the strain of overtime, second shifts, expanded management teams, and other cost pressures.

Cost pressures on earnings expectations further increase toward the latter part of Stage II. Labor and raw materials costs continue to rise. Bottlenecks, imbalances, and shortages occur in labor and raw materials. Bidding wars for labor and raw materials break out. Third production shifts, still more costly to train and less efficient, are hired to meet demand for goods and services. Middle-and senior-management teams expand. Productivity and profit margins fall. The rate of increase in expected earnings growth in the numerator of the Equation (3) valuation framework grinds toward a halt.

Simultaneously the rate of increase in interest rates accelerates. At the beginning of Stage II, interest rates are rising slightly. The trough in economic activity has passed. The economy is expanding. The demand for money in the normal course of economic expansion increases. Consumer confidence and spending also increase. The Fed might "lean against the wind" and slow the rate of growth in the money supply. An accelerating rate of increase in interest rates heightens risk in the Equation (3) valuation framework denominator. However, the rate of increase in expected earnings of the numerator of the Equation (3) valuation framework remains greater. Common stock prices continue to rise. The rate of that rise is less than the rapid rise of Stage I because investors are now in combination 8a from Table 1.1. Both expected earnings and interest rates are increasing. However, expected earnings are still increasing more rapidly than interest rates.

Interest rates continue to increase at an accelerating rate as Stage

II progresses. Economic expansion gains more forward momentum. Consumer confidence and spending increase further. Business spending increases in response to the expanding economy. Travel, promotional, and other business expenses expand. The demand for money further expands.

Prices become firm. Companies that previously could not raise prices because of overcapacity in their industries comfortably raise prices. The price increases are an effort to return to the highest profit margins of the cycle experienced during Stage I. Those highest profit margins have shrunk as Stage II progresses because the extremely lean operating conditions of Stage I have disappeared. The second shifts and enlarged middle management hired to meet rising demand are not as efficient as the first, core shift and smaller management teams of Stage I. Firms attempt to boost profit margins, despite lower productivity, by raising prices. The Fed smells the incipient signs of an unacceptable level of inflation. Money supply growth is slowed. Interest rates rise.

The rate of increase in interest rates accelerates beyond that experienced earlier in Stage II. The denominator of the Equation (3) valuation framework rises faster but still not as fast as the more slowly growing expected earnings in the numerator of the Equation (3) valuation framework. Common stock prices continue to rise but more slowly compared to earlier in Stage II and in Stage I. Investors remain in combination 8a of Table 1.1. However, the rate of growth in expected earnings has slowed. The rate of increase in interest rates has accelerated, although it remains below that of the slowed rate of increase in expected earnings.

Toward the end of Stage II, the rate of growth in interest rates accelerates more rapidly. The demand for money becomes much larger. The rate of growth in the money supply slows or may drop. The corporate demand for money, previously subdued because of overcapacity, spurts. Corporations that previously would not consider capital expenditures, particularly for expansion, almost in unison initiate large capital investments. The demand for their goods and services has finally surpassed their production capability. Large capital expenditures, in excess of internally-generated funds, spark a significant demand for money. Meanwhile the Fed has decreased the rate of growth or absolutely decreased the money supply as it fears higher inflation. Interest rates rise relatively more rapidly than earlier in Stage II.

Interest rates in the last part of Stage II accelerate faster not only in response to the relatively sudden, large revival in corporate demand for money but also in response to consumer demand for money. In this last part of Stage II, consumers are demanding and spending considerably more money. Consumers are now accustomed to prosperity. Their assets have grown, and they broaden their spending. Consumers spend on luxury items that they previously were not confident enough, or had not saved enough, to buy. With common stock prices at new highs, the "wealth effect" kicks in. Consumers now buy jewelry, cruises, and other luxury items. Consumer replacement demand for worn durables, such as cars, reignites. Money demand is now compounded by both the resurgence in corporate and consumer demand for money.

Prices are rising more rapidly than ever in the growing prosperity of the last part of Stage II. Demand may exceed the supply of goods and services. Demand/pull inflation occurs in the process of allocating the limited supply of goods and services. Supply bottlenecks and other imbalances appear. Prices jump. The purchasing power risk premium component in interest rates increases. The Fed responds vigorously. Money supply growth slows or drops. The compound effect of higher prices and more demand than supply for money forces rapidly increasing interest rates.

The rate of increase in interest rates in the denominator of the Equation (3) valuation framework starts to catch up quickly with the rate of increase in expected earnings. But common stock prices continue to increase slowly *until* the rate of increase in interest rates and the rate of growth in expected earnings are equal. The stock market reaches a cycle high at the end of Stage II, as denoted by H in Figure 3.1.

Common stock prices reach their high for this economic/stock price cycle in combination 8c of Table 1.1. The rate of increase in expected earnings equals the rate of increase in interest rates. The rates of change in the numerator and denominator of the Equation (3) valuation framework are equal. Investors know only in hindsight when this has occurred. Surrounded by swirling changes in earnings expectations, interest rates, and other contradictory and confusing signs as the economy is about to launch its final ascent to its peak, investors usually cannot definitely identify the high in common stock prices at the very time it happens. Yet it assuredly happens.

Stage II and the high in common stock prices for this economic/

stock price cycle come to an end before the expansion in economic activity ends. Interest rates, pushed up by the tighter demand/supply for money and the higher purchasing power risk premiums from inflation, overtake the rate of increase in expected earnings even though they are still rising, albeit more slowly.

The signs that accompany the high in common stock prices are usually confusing and contradictory at the time. Bullish signs usually include still rising expected earnings, although they are slowed. Strong consumer demand continues. Business capital expenditure plans are strong because production capacity is strained. Yet common stock prices reach their high because the rate at which expected earnings are discounted now equals the rate of growth in those expected earnings. Earnings growth is now exactly negated by the rate of discount. The high in common stock prices, denoted by H in Figure 3.1, has been reached for this cycle.

STAGE III

The downturn in common stock prices starts at the beginning of Stage III, although the economy and interest rates continue upward. Employment, personal income, and consumer confidence remain high. Consumer demand for goods and services continues to be high. Supply bottlenecks and imbalances occur. Marginal productivity declines. Concern about faltering stock prices rises. However, the economy remains relatively robust and certainly not in a recession despite pressure on expected earnings.

Interest rates increase at an accelerating rate, exerting more downward pressure on stock prices. The demand for money remains strong. Consumers and corporations continue to borrow. Corporations are in the middle of a large capital-spending boom. Their demand for money to finance expansions and modernization is high. The supply of money is tight and getting tighter. The Fed slows or contracts the money supply to fight inflation.

Inflation is at its zenith. The economy is strong. The demand for goods and services exceeds supply. Prices are easily raised. The purchasing power risk premium is larger, causing interest rates to increase further. The rate of increase in expected earnings is lower than the rate of increase in interest rates. Common stock prices decline. This is combination 8b from Table 1.1. Now both bond prices and stock prices are declining. This combination continues to the peak in economic activity, as denoted by P in Figure 3.1.

Lower free reserves are observed as financial institutions stretch credit-quality criteria at the cyclical peak while the money supply slows or contracts. The yield curve flattens and later inverts. Investors tend to ignore these signs and push price/earnings multiples unrealistically high, anticipating expected earnings growth well beyond logical time horizons (discussed in Chapter 7).

The signs of the impending common stock price decline are obvious after the peak in economic activity and the substantial decline in common stock prices. Investors look back and see that the boom was unsustainable. The economy was growing too fast for its capacity. Inflation was distorting the allocation of goods and services, etcetera.

STAGE IV

The worst of the decreasing earnings expectations and rising interest rates (combination 7 from Table 1.1) occurs after the peak in economic activity. Lags in information, ordering and production scheduling, incorrect sales forecasts, etc. cause inventory to arrive after the peak in economic activity. Capital spending on new plant and equipment presses toward completion. However, the anticipated sales for which the inventory and the plant and equipment were ordered do not materialize. Sales forecasts, based on the rising sales incurred during the expansion, are too high. Inventory accumulates. Costs rise. Prices are slashed to reduce unanticipated inventory accumulation. Profit margins shrink. Outlays for new plant and equipment continue because few firms will or can immediately stop construction or modernization spending upon the first sign of a slowdown. Accounts receivable collection slows, particularly among the marginal accounts that looked creditworthy under the brighter economic conditions of a few months before. Collection costs increase, further decreasing expected earnings.

The steepest rate of decrease in expected earnings occurs in the period after the peak in economic activity, as denoted by P in Figure 1.1. The prices at which the goods and services can be sold are flat or declining while the costs of the goods and services are at cycle highs. The goods were ordered at suppliers' peak pricing power. Inventory and accounts receivable are at their highest for the cycle and must be carried longer at high interest rates.

Interest rates continue rising sharply even after the peak in economic activity. The Fed is still vigorously fighting inflation. The money supply is tight. Lenders become more selective as delinquencies emerge. Yet the demand for money continues to be strong and rising for a short time after the economic peak. Firms demand money to finance unanticipated inventory accumulation, the slowing accounts receivable collection, and completion of the large capital-expenditure projects undertaken late in the economic expansion. A credit squeeze or crunch may occur. Interest rates spike. The fastest rate of increase in interest rates during the economic/stock price cycle occurs.

The combination of the largest rate of decrease in expected earnings and the fastest rate of increase in interest rates during the cycle occurs in early Stage IV. This simultaneous confluence of the two most depressing influences on common stock prices causes a steep drop in common stock prices. The numerator in the Equation (3) valuation framework declines rapidly. The denominator in the Equation (3) valuation framework increases rapidly. Common stock prices fall rapidly.

Signs of faltering and then declining common stock prices appear ambiguous early in Stage III but obvious in Stage IV. The first signs may be anecdotal since the more formal statistical data are delayed in collection and compilation. A quick survey of neighborhood car dealership lots may show signs of bulging inventory since consumer durables are among the first goods to stop selling. Credit quality deteriorates, reflecting the extension of credit to less creditworthy borrowers in the euphoria at the economic cycle peak and the slower payments from those borrowers after the peak. Less credit is extended. Sales decline further.

Common stock prices decline throughout Stage IV. The recession deepens. Expected earnings drop sharply immediately after the peak in economic activity. Prices are slashed to work off the unanticipated, accumulated inventory. Higher costs, particularly those associated with inventory financing and falling productivity, must also be worked off.

Expected earnings continue to decrease, even after their initial sharp drop and efforts to restore profits, but at a now decreasing rate of decline. Firms cut costs, inventory, less creditworthy accounts, employees, etc. in an attempt to stem the profit slide and restore profit margins. The fixed costs embedded in the operating structures during the economic boom, however, decline slowly as the recession grinds on. Severance pay may be incurred as the number of employees is reduced. The partially-finished plants and equipment installations are most likely completed during the earlier phases of Stage IV. Completion is more likely than abandonment since the older, less efficient plants can be closed as capacity is cut back in the recession. The costs of the new plants and the closing of the old plants must be digested in earnings before the decline in expected profits can be stemmed. The recession worsens. Cost-cutting efforts are offset by decreasing sales.

Interest rates are at first slow to decline or may continue to climb in the beginning of Stage IV. The demand for money remains strong for a while. Companies finance the unanticipated inventory accumulation and the completion of capital-spending projects for which internal funds have decreased. The money supply decreases because the Fed is vigorously fighting inflation. This supply/demand imbalance for money temporarily supports high interest rates.

After the typical spike in short-term interest rates at the end of Stage III and into the early Stage IV, the demand for money slows as consumers and businesses curtail spending. The supply of money reverses course and starts to grow as the Fed recognizes the worsening recession. A cautious Fed may initially increase the money supply and cut interest rates slowly. A less cautious Fed may flood the economy with liquidity, planting the seeds for the next round of boom and bust in the economic/stock price cycle.

The decline in expected earnings continues but at a decreasing rate. The decrease in interest rates continues but at an increasing rate. In terms of the Equation (3) valuation framework, the expected earnings in the numerator are decreasing more rapidly than interest rates in the denominator. This is combination 9a from Table 1.1. Common stock prices decline further but at a decreasing rate.

The rate of decrease in expected earnings eventually declines to a point equal to the rate of decrease in interest rates. The cycle low in stock prices has been reached at the end of Stage IV, as denoted by L in Figure 3.1. The Equation (3) valuation framework numerator and denominator are declining at the same rate of decrease. This is combination 9c in Table 1.1. Common stock prices reverse course after their low. The processes of the economic/stock price cycle regenerate. The next cycle occurs.

How long do the different combinations of Table 1.1 usually last?

While the combinations of Table 1.1 occur over the economic/ stock price cycle in the sequence described above, the length and magnitude of each combination varies considerably among cycles. Much of the variation arises from the variation in the economic cycle. Some recessions have lasted only a few months. Some expansions have lasted many years.

The rising phase of common stock prices (Stages I and II) lasts the longest among the various combinations of Table 1.1. Interest rates remain stable at relatively low levels after the stock market has turned up from its low. The small demand for money and large supply of it during the end of the expansion and the beginning of the economic recovery keep interest rates down. Only after the expansion is fully underway does the demand for money start to exert upward pressure on interest rates. Upward inflation pressures appear only after the demand for goods and services has worked through excess production capacity later in the economic expansion. The increased demands for both money and goods and services take time to develop and gather momentum. Meanwhile expected earnings are rising rapidly.

The rise in common stock prices ends relatively quickly, upon entering Stage III, with a spurt in interest rates and much slower expected earnings growth. The Fed may come to realize, after the fact, that it must act to counter inflation. It does so with intent to "catch up." The Fed's tightening may be relatively severe. Borrowers rush to secure funds as interest rates rise rapidly. More imbalances and supply bottlenecks in the economy emerge. Higher prices ripple throughout the economy. Common stock prices top and then drop. Stage III is usually relatively short. The severe Fed medicine takes hold. Economic activity drops abruptly. The ensuing bear market reflects the abrupt change. Common stock prices plummet.

The Fed historically overresponds with an easing in the money supply and interest rates as the economy falters and unemployment rises in the Stage IV recession. The urgency and magnitude of the Fed response are fast and large. Liquidity floods the markets. Most of the increased money supply first enters the stock and bond markets. Common stock prices hit their low and rebound. The quick, large infusion of liquidity directly entering the stock market causes the Stage IV duration of declining stock prices to be relatively short in comparison to the extended Stage I and II rising stock price phases of the cycle. The ebbs and flows in monetary liquidity make the falling phase of common stock prices relatively short and the rising phase of common stock prices relatively long. Bull markets usually last longer than bear markets.

VISUAL HISTORY

The Federal Reserve Bank of St. Louis charts of the annual rates of change in the Standard and Poor's 500 Index, corporate profits, the Consumer Price Index, and levels of interest rates (Exhibit 3.1) provide an approximate visualization of the historical relationships among the causal factors in the Equation (3) valuation framework.

A visual examination reveals a pattern among the causal factors in bull and bear common stock markets that fits the Equation (3) valuation framework. Rising rates of expected earnings precede bull markets and falling or relatively stable interest rates accompanying them. This pattern accompanied rising stock prices in 1975, 1980, 1983, 1989, and 1995–middle 1999. Falling rates of expected earnings precede bear markets and rising inflation and interest rates accompany them. This pattern accompanied declining common stock prices in 1974, 1977–1978, 1981–1982, 1987, and 1990.

SUMMARY

Interaction between expected earnings and interest rates within the Equation (3) valuation framework causes common stock price fluctuations. The relative rates of change in each of these causal factors drive the direction and speed of change, summarized in the combinations of Table 1.1. The typical progression over the economic/stock price cycle can be divided into four distinct stages:

STAGE I. Common stock prices hit their lows shortly before the trough in economic activity when the rate of change in expected earnings equals the rate of change in interest rates. Expected earnings, responding to the anticipated economic recovery, begin to rise while interest rates are still declining or flat. Common stock prices rise. The divergence between rising expected earnings and declining or flat interest rates is greatest in early Stage 1, leading to the most rapid rise in common stock prices of the stock price cycle. Common stock prices rise throughout Stage 1 as the rate of increase in expected earnings outpaces the rate of increase in interest rates.

STAGE II. Rising common stock prices continue as long as the rate of increase in the expected earnings exceeds the rate of increase in interest rates. The rate of increase in expected earnings slows and the rate of increase in interest rates accelerates throughout this stage.

Exhibit 3.1
Visual History of the Equation (3) Valuation Framework

Standard and Poor's 500 Index with Reinvested Dividends

Interest Rates

Exhibit 3.1 (*continued*)

Consumer Price Index

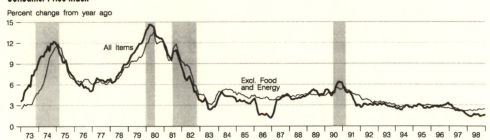

Corporate Profits after Tax (with IVA and CCAdj)

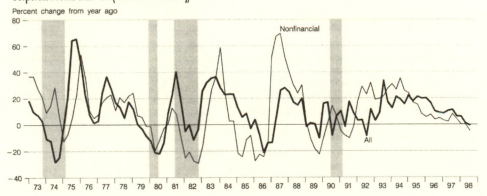

Source: National Economic Trends Federal Reserve Bank of St. Louis

47

Common stock prices reach their highs when the rate of increase in expected earnings equals the rate of increase in interest rates.

STAGE III. The common stock bear market starts when the rate of increase in expected earnings is less than the rate of increase in interest rates. Interest rates rise rapidly while investors simultaneously anticipate an increasingly pronounced slowing in the rate of increase in expected earnings throughout Stage III.

STAGE IV. Interest rates, particularly on short-term maturities, rise rapidly and may spike in a credit crunch as the economic/stock price cycle enters Stage IV. Expected earnings decrease sharply at first in Stage IV. Falling common stock prices accelerate.

Further into Stage IV, typical recession effects emerge. Interest rates decrease as the imbalance in the demand for money and supply of it eases and disappears toward the latter part of Stage IV. Expected earnings continue to decrease but at a slower rate. That rate of decrease in expected earnings is greater than the rate of decrease in interest rates. Common stock prices continue to fall but not as rapidly.

The low in common stock prices is reached when the rates of decrease in expected earnings and interest rates are equal. The common stock price cycle reenters its upward phase when the rate of decrease in the expected earnings is less than the rate of decrease in interest rates.

The length and magnitude of the stages vary just as the length and magnitude of economic cycles vary. Bear market phases of the cycles have been shorter than bull market phases. The common stock price trend has been upward. Each successive bull market has carried common stock prices to new highs.

Appendix 3A

The Yield Curve

The pattern of different yields on bonds of equal quality but different maturities is the yield curve. Traditional yield curve configurations are based on the directional slope of the observed pattern moving from the shortest to the longest maturity. U.S. Treasury bonds most often represent the yield curve because of their uniform, highest quality, default-free risk. Inflation-indexed and other nontraditional U.S. Treasuries are usually excluded from the yield curve because of their unique provisions. The yield curve is also known as the term structure of interest rates.

UPWARD SLOPING

Yields on the upward-sloping yield curve move increasingly higher as maturities lengthen. Short-term money market instruments, such as U.S. Treasury bills, have the lowest yields. Intermediate-term maturities have higher yields. Long-term maturities have the highest yields. The general configuration is upward, although probably not in uniform increments from one maturity to the next and not in a perfectly straight line.

FLAT

The flat yield curve is relatively horizontal over all maturities. The U.S. Treasury bill, the thirty-year U.S. Treasury bond, and all maturities in between have approximately the same yield. Although the totally flat yield curve is rarely observed, the general configuration is horizontal. The flat yield curve implies expected stable inflation, economic activity, and interest rates.

DOWNWARD (INVERTED) SLOPING

Yields on the downward-sloping yield curve move increasingly lower as maturity lengthens. Short-term yields are higher than intermediate-term yields which in turn, are higher than long-term yields. This yield curve configuration is the inverse of the upward sloping and is sometimes called the inverted yield curve.

YIELD CURVE IMPLICATIONS

Different slopes of the yield curve have different implications for the economic/stock price cycle. Investors infer economic expansion and growing earnings from an upward-sloping yield curve. As long as the slope is not very steep, the expected associated increases in inflation and interest rates are relatively mild and "normal." Expected earnings growth is supported by the expansion. The rate of increase in the expected earnings numerator of the Equation (3) valuation framework exceeds the rate of increase in the required rate of return in the denominator. The economic/stock price cycle is in the latter part of Stage I or in Stage II.

The economic boom, at some point, may cause interest rates along the entire upward-sloping yield curve to rise rapidly enough to overpower the expected earnings growth. The expected increases in inflation and interest rates may no longer be "mild." The relationship between the numerator and the denominator of the Equation (3) valuation framework reverses. Expected earnings are rising less rapidly than interest rates. Common stock prices fall. The economic/stock price cycle is at the end of Stage II.

The inverted yield curve usually occurs when the demand for money surpasses supply. The economy may have unexpectedly and abruptly slowed. A rush to finance unintended inventory accumulation and swelling accounts receivable runs headlong into the Fed's wall of tight money. The classic credit crunch arrives. Short-term interest rates gush upward and surpass long-term interest rates that now incorporate recession expectations. The yield curve inverts. Common stock prices fall. Expected earnings in the numerator of the Equation (3) valuation framework decline. The rate of increase in the required rate of return in the denominator accelerates. Common stock prices fall. The economic/stock price cycle is in Stage IV.

After a relatively brief credit squeeze, the yield curve settles into a more gently downward-sloping to flat posture throughout the rest of the recession. Investors infer economic slowdown or recession from a downward-sloping yield curve. Lower interest rates are anticipated as the demand for money diminishes during the economic recession. The Fed expands the money supply. The inflation rate decreases. Deflation may occur in a severe case. Expected earnings slow or decline. The rate of decrease in expected earnings in the numerator of the Equation (3) valuation framework exceeds the rate of decline in interest rates in the denominator. The economic/stock price cycle remains in Stage IV.

The yield curve may flatten or regain a mild upward slope as the economic/stock price cycle leaves Stage IV and reenters Stage I. The recession slides through the last phases of Stage IV into Stage I of the next economic expansion. Early in Stage I, investors recognize the passage, and the yield curve is again upward sloping.

YIELD CURVE INCREMENTS

Clues to expected interest rates might be contained in the incremental yield as maturity lengthens. From one maturity on the yield curve to the next, the difference in yield between each longer maturity may widen in response to investor expectations of more quickly rising or more slowly falling interest rates. Conversely the incremental difference in yield between each longer maturity may narrow in response to investor expectations of more slowly rising or more rapidly falling interest rates.

YIELD SPREAD

The yield spread is the difference between bonds of the same maturity but different quality. Lower-quality bonds have higher yields. The higher-quality bond, usually the U.S. Treasury bond, has the lower yield. The higher-quality bond yield is subtracted from the lower-quality bond yield to derive the yield spread.

As the yield spread narrows, investors infer an optimistic view of the economy. Bond investors are more confident lower-quality issuers will generate sufficient cash flow to meet their debt service. Investors sacrifice quality to garner extra yield. Narrowing yield spreads most often occur in Stage II and III of the economic/stock price cycle.

Widening yield spreads indicate a pessimistic economic outlook. Bond investors are less confident lower-quality issuers will meet debt service and sacrifice yield for quality. Widening yield spreads most often occur in Stage IV of the economic/stock price cycle.

FUTURE CONTRACTS IMPLIED INTEREST RATES

Future contracts on debt securities and Fed funds contain implied future interest rates. Prevailing implications can change as bond and other debt contract prices change.

INFLATION INDICATION

The difference between the yield on the inflation-indexed U.S. Treasury bond and the traditional U.S. Treasury bond of the same maturity that has no inflation protection may imply the expected rate of inflation. Investors may use this in the Equation (3) valuation framework and other analysis.

4

Portfolio Asset Allocation Implications

Are there implications for portfolio asset allocation in the combinations of Table 1.1 and in Figure 3.1?

Periods within the economic/stock price cycle depicted in Figure 3.1 have returns on common stocks higher than those of either long-term U.S. Treasury bonds or money market securities. Conversely other periods within the economic/stock price cycle have returns on long-term U.S. Treasury bonds or money market securities higher than those of common stocks. Investors who use assets allocation to divide their portfolios among the three traditional, security categories of common stocks, long-term U.S. Treasury bonds, and money market securities (cash) base their subjective allocation decisions on their envisioned, current location in the economic/stock price cycle.

WHEN TO EMPHASIZE COMMON STOCKS

Investors want greater portfolio allocation in common stocks during Stages I and II in Figure 3.1 when common stock prices rise from their lows to their highs for the current stock price cycle. These stages are associated with the combinations of Table 1.1 when the expected earnings in the numerator of the Equation (3) valuation framework are rising more rapidly (after the trough in economic activity in Stage I and Stage II) or declining more slowly (early Stage I before the economic trough) than interest rates in the denominator.

Interest rates usually rise throughout Stages I and II except possibly briefly between the low in common stock prices and the trough in economic activity in the economic/stock price cycle. Long-term bond prices fall. Money market securities retain their value and receive increasingly higher yields as the economic expansion pressures short-term interest rates higher. However, their stable principal does not participate in the common stock bull market of Stages I and II. Although returning more than long-term bonds, money market securities are not the highest return asset allocation in Stages I and II. Common stocks are the highest return asset allocation in these Stages.

WHEN TO EMPHASIZE MONEY MARKET SECURITIES

A portfolio asset allocation that emphasizes money market securities is most desirable when both common stock and long-term bond prices are falling. This simultaneous decline occurs between the high in common stock prices reached at the end of Stage II in Figure 3.1 and the most severe credit tightening, possibly a squeeze or crunch, of the economic/stock price cycle reached shortly after the peak in economic activity at the end of Stage III or in early Stage IV.

Common stock prices experience the most precipitous part of their fall in late Stage III and early Stage IV. Expected earnings decline sharply. The numerator in the Equation (3) valuation framework falls. At the same time interest rates rise and may spike sharply. Fed-supplied liquidity is curtailed. Demand for money remains high. Long-term bond prices fall. The denominator in the Equation (3) valuation framework rises rapidly. This reflects combination 7, the most bearish for common stock prices, from Table 1.1.

Investors do not want to be in common stocks or in long-term bonds in Stage III or early Stage IV. Both securities are losing value at their most rapid rate in these periods of the economic/stock price cycle. Money market securities offer the only positive return to be garnered over this relatively short span in the cycle. Money market securities do not lose value and still have a positive return. Common stocks and long-term bonds have negative returns.

WHEN TO EMPHASIZE LONG-TERM BONDS

An asset allocation should emphasize long-term U.S. Treasury bonds in most of Stage IV, after any credit crunch at the beginning of the stage. Between the spike in interest rates at the end of Stage III and early Stage IV and the low in common stock prices at the end of Stage IV, interest rates decline and long-term U.S. Treasury bond prices rise (interest rates fall). The lower interest rates reflect slowing and/or declining economic activity, higher Fed money supply, lower consumer and business demand for money, and less inflation.

Lower-quality bonds may not feel this upward price pressure. Lower-quality, higher-default risk bonds may still be viewed with apprehension. Their default risk may have been underappreciated by investors during the economic expansion of the prior Stages in the economic/stock price cycle. Their default risk may now be overappreciated. The prices of lower-quality bonds continue to decline even after the incipient earnings recovery and despite lower interest rates. Bond investors remain fearful these issuers may not revive in time, if at all, to meet looming debt service. The price reaction of lower-quality bonds varies directly with the severity of their default risk.

While long-term U.S. Treasury bond prices are rising during most of Stage IV, common stock prices and yields on money market securities are falling. The declining economic activity associated with Stage IV causes expected earnings to drop, albeit at a slower rate of decrease as this Stage progresses. The rate of decline in expected earnings remains greater than the rate of decline in interest rates throughout Stage IV in Figure 3.1. Expected earnings in the numerator of the Equation (3) valuation framework decline at a faster rate than interest rates in the denominator. This combination 9a from Table 1.1 causes common stock prices to decline throughout Stage IV. Asset allocation should emphasize long-term U.S. Treasury bonds during most of Stage IV after any credit crunch early in the Stage.

WHEN TO SELL SHORT

Aggressive asset allocation includes short selling common stocks and long-term U.S. Treasury bonds. Common stocks are most profitably sold short at the high in common stock prices, at the beginning of Stage III, and positions held through the end of Stage IV, the low in the common stock price cycle. Common stock prices decline as the economic/stock price cycle progresses throughout these two Stages, as depicted in Figure 3.1.

Long-term U.S. Treasury bonds are most profitably sold short at, or relatively soon after, the trough in economic activity in early Stage I, shortly after the low in stock prices. Lags in data and Fed reaction cause delays between the exact moment of the economic trough and interest rates. The Fed may continue to fight the recession even after the trough because it is unaware the trough has occurred until it analyzes delayed data. Short positions in long-term bonds are most profitably covered shortly after the peak in economic activity, usually characterized by a credit squeeze or crunch and spiking interest rates.

ECONOMIC/STOCK PRICE CYCLE SIDELIGHTS

Common Stocks as Inflation Hedges

Common stocks have often been thought of as inflation hedges because expected earnings can outpace inflation. The prices of goods and services could be increased at the same or faster rate than general inflation. The prices that the firm charged would rise sufficiently to offset cost increases. Profit margins would be stable or increasing. As dollar sales rose, expected corporate earnings rose because the same or higher profit margin applied to higher-dollar sales. As long as the firm could raise its selling prices as fast or faster than its costs, profits continued to rise faster than inflation. Firms maintained or even widened their profit margins during the inflationary periods in the second half of the twentieth century. Their profits rose. Their common stock prices rose. Common stocks were regarded as inflation hedges.

The common stock inflation hedge characteristics conform to the Equation (3) valuation framework. Common stock prices outpace inflation as long as the rate of increase in the expected earnings numerator exceeds the rate of increase caused by inflation in the interest rates of the denominator.

Common stock prices fall if the rate of increase in expected earnings is less than the rate of increase in interest rates caused by inflation. The impact of the late 1970s oil embargo illustrates this. A bear market, except for oil stocks, occurred as historically high inflation caused interest rates to soar to historically high levels. Only oil companies were able to raise product prices sufficiently to offset increased costs. Most other firms could not raise prices because so much more of consumer and corporate income was being spent on oil and energy.

Most firms, except for oil companies, met resistance to price increases while paying higher costs. Their profit margins shrunk. Their stock prices declined. The common stock prices of oil companies, however, rose because their expected earnings were rising more rapidly than the rapidly rising rates. Oil companies' expected earnings in the numerator of the Equation (3) valuation framework were rising at a faster rate than interest rates in the denominator.

The conception of common stocks as inflation hedges had to be tempered. Common stocks are only inflation hedges when the rate of increase in expected earnings induced by inflation exceeds the rate of increase in interest rates also induced by inflation.

Hyperinflation has led to extraordinarily high interest rates and total collapses of corporate profits, currencies and entire economies since the days of the Roman Empire. In terms of the Equation (3) valuation framework, expected earnings cannot achieve a sustainable, fast-enough rate of increase to exceed the rate of increase in interest rates. Common stock prices fall. Economies afflicted by hyperinflation usually regress to barter, political unrest and collapse, and sometimes, armed conflict. Investors flee. Corporations and common stock prices crumble in that environment. Common stocks are not a hyperinflation hedge.

Bond and Stock Price Linkage

Bond and stock prices are sometimes linked. Rising bond prices (declining interest rates) and rising common stock prices are seen as partners in bull markets. Declining stock prices and bond prices (rising interest rates) are partners in bear markets. This occurred in many years of the 1980s and 1990s when a relatively unique confluence of low and declining inflation and interest rates during economic expansion accompanied a rise in corporate efficiency and earnings. This is not the typical combination. Interest rates usually rise during economic expansion.

The link between bond and stock prices is expected only in Stage III and possibly in early Stage I. Bond and common stock prices should be unlinked in the other periods of the economic/stock price cycle (Exhibit 4.1).

The link between higher bond prices (lower interest rates) and higher common stock prices may occur relatively fleetingly in the beginning of Stage I, around the low in common stock prices, and in Stage III. In the beginning of Stage I, expected earnings are declining very slowly or rebounding while the economy remains in a recession

Exhibit 4.1
Bond and Stock Price Linkage

Stage I   Unlinked (except possibly in early Stage I)
Stage II   Unlinked
Stage III   Linked
Stage IV   Unlinked

that the Fed is still fighting with lower interest rates and a growing money supply. Rebounding expected earnings and stable interest rates at low levels (flat bond prices) that are possibly heading slightly lower (slightly higher bond prices) are combined. The link between higher bond prices (lower interest rates) and higher common stock prices may be fleetingly observed.

Lower bond prices (higher interest rates) and common stock prices are again typically linked in Stage III. Interest rates are high and rising. Their rate of increase exceeds the rate of increase in expected earnings. Bond and common stock prices decline. Lower bond prices (higher interest rates) are the partner of lower stock prices.

Bond and common stock prices are unlinked in most of Stage I and all of Stages II and IV. Expanding economic activity in Stage I, after the economic trough, and in Stage II exerts upward pressure on both expected earnings and interest rates. The rates of increase in expected earnings is greater than the rate on increase in interest rates. This is combination 8a from Table 1.1. Common stock prices rise and bond prices fall throughout most of Stage I and all of Stage II.

Bond and common stock prices are unlinked in Stage IV. The recession induces higher bond prices (lower interest rates) and lower common stock prices. This unlinked relationship occurs because the rate of decrease in expected earnings exceeds the rate of decrease in interest rates. This unlinked relationship continues as long as the rate of decrease in expected earnings exceeds the rate of decrease in interest rates, as reflected in combination 9a from Table 1.1. This unlinked relationship conforms to the Equation (3) valuation framework.

This combination of simultaneously rising common stock and bond prices (lower interest rates) is not reflected in the typical relationship between economic activity on one hand and interest rates and earnings on the other. A recession with higher interest rates is not normally anticipated. Recessions are more often associated with lower interest rates. The late 1970s and early 1980s extraordinary cost/push of oil prices caused a relatively unique combination of high inflation, high interest rates and recession-induced lower expected earnings. Add the Fed's strong, tightening response to wring inflation, and common stock prices plummeted along with bond prices in 1981. Market observers and financial commentators linked lower bond prices (higher interest rates) with lower stock prices.

In 1983 and into the mid-1980s, oil prices plummeted. Cost/push deflation caused interest rates to decline while expected earnings rebounded sharply (except for oil companies). The combination of declining interest rates (rising bond prices) and rising expected earnings caused common stock prices to surge. Again investors observed an unusual confluence of higher expected earnings, caused by an economic expansion, combining with unexpectedly declining interest rates during that expansion. This reflects combination 2 from Table 1.1 and conforms to the Equation (3) valuation framework.

Market observers correctly linked higher expected earnings and lower interest rates as the tandem partners pushing up common stock prices in 1983 and mid-1984. Yet this is not the typically anticipated behavior of interest rates over the mostly expansionary Stage I and Stage II in the economic/stock price cycle.

The more typically anticipated pattern of unlinked falling bond prices and rising stock prices returned in the latter part of 1983. In the last part of 1983, bond prices fell (interest rates rose) while common stock prices rose. This unlinked pattern is typical throughout most of Stages I and II.

Bond and common stock prices relinked in the mid-1980s as plummeting oil prices caused inflation and interest rates to decline unexpectedly during an economic expansion while expected earnings rose, as usual, during that economic expansion.[2]

In late 1987 interest rates, which had started to rise in August 1987, spurted in response to demand/pull inflationary indications and a diligent, precautionary Fed tightening. Interest rates spiked as typically anticipated at the end of a bull market. The rate of increase in interest rates exceeded the rate of increase in expected earnings. True to the Equation (3) valuation framework, the bull market ended and, in fact, crashed. Lower bond prices (higher interest rates) and lower common stock prices linked as usually anticipated in Stage III.

The bear market of late 1987 was relatively short-lived as Fed monetary tightening was quickly replaced with loosening. Interest rates moved lower, liquidity rose, expected earnings moved upward, and common stock prices rebounded. The burst of Fed liquidity kept interest rates low and slightly falling through most of 1988. Investors observed a typical Table 1.1, combination 2, common stock bull market. Bond and common stock prices linked in typical early Stage I fashion.

The typical economic/stock price cycle returned after the oil embargo inflation shock and the large Fed money supply loosening waned. As the economy expanded in late 1989 and early 1990, expected earnings and interest rates increased. Bond prices fell and common stock prices rose. The normally anticipated unlinked pattern typically observed in most of Stage I and Stage II returned. Market observers now commented that the linkage between lower interest rates (higher bond prices) and higher stock prices had been broken. Yet this was the unlinked pattern of the economic/stock price cycles from 1950 through most of the 1970s, before the oil shock distortions. Interest rates and common stock prices are typically unlinked during most of Stage I and Stage II.

Bond prices generally rose (interest rates fell) in the 1990–1991 recession. Expected earnings first fell and then recovered. Common stock prices first fell while bond prices rose (interest rates fell). Common stock prices rose in the latter part of the recession, when expected earnings recovered, while bond prices rose (interest rates fell). Investors again witnessed the typical unlinked bond and common stock price pattern expected in Stage IV and the typical linked pattern in early Stage I.

In the strong bull market of the middle and late 1990s, the link between higher bond prices (lower interest rates) and higher stock prices reappeared. Little, if any, inflation and government budget surpluses combined with a reenergized corporate cost-cutting effort to simultaneously induce lower interest rates and higher expected earnings. Markets again observed the linkage of higher bond prices (lower interest rates) and higher common stock prices. This linked partnership conforms to the Equation (3) valuation framework and reflects combination 2 of Table 1.1. It is not the typically anticipated pattern of bond and common stock prices over the economic expansion associated with most of Stage I and Stage II in the typical economic/ stock price cycle.

Time will reveal whether bond and common stock price linkage will be the future norm or a few decades of exception. The last decades of the twentieth century have seen mostly bull markets caused by simultaneously low and declining interest rates (higher bond prices) and high and rising expected earnings during an economic expansion (combination 2 from Table 1.1). This combination is the most conducive to common stock bull markets.

Causes for the unanticipated bullish parallel movement in bond and common stock prices observed in Stages I and II could range from technology-driven efficiency to improved management and employee productivity, etc. The effect could be temporary or lasting. The odds favor a return to the more typically unlinked behavior of bond and common stock prices over most of the economic/stock price cycle, except in Stage III and possibly in early Stage I.

Fed Policy

The same Fed policy has different impacts on common stock prices depending on the current location in the economic/stock price cycle. A relatively rapid Fed-induced increase in the money supply and liquidity is bullish at and after the low in common stock prices of early Stage I. The first impact of the Fed loosening at this point in the economic/stock price cycle encourages the purchase of financial rather than tangible assets. Interest rates decline. The increased money supply exceeds the slack demand for money. The denominator in the Equation (3) valuation framework decreases. Common stock prices rise. Continued Fed increases in the money supply through Stage I and most of Stage II will be bullish for common stocks because interest rate increases are slowed. However, further Fed loosening turns bearish at some point before the high in stock prices.

If the Fed continues to loosen monetary policy and increase the money supply as financial markets progress toward and into Stage III, the converse impact occurs. The increased money supply impact changes to increased upward pressures on interest rates and downward pressures on common stock prices. Investors envision high money supply growth as fertilizer in a field ready to grow inflation. The demand for goods and services has grown and starts to strain supply. Too much money may be chasing too few goods and services. The specter of demand/pull inflation emerges. Interest rates rise. Eventually the rate of increase in interest rates caused by loosening Fed monetary policy exceeds the rate of increase in expected earnings.

Common stock prices fall. Continued Fed loosening only exacerbates inflation, raises interest rates, and deepens the common stock bear market through the peak in economic activity.

The same loose Fed policy of a relatively rapid increase in the money supply will, conversely, be bullish for common stock prices after the peak, through the trough in economic activity and into Stages I and II. The loose Fed policy exerts further and speedier downward pressure on interest rates that, in turn, fosters higher common stock prices.

Tightening Fed policy has different impacts at different points in the economic/stock price cycle. Tightening during the recession or at the trough, as depicted in Figure 3.1, prolongs the bear market in common stocks. Conversely, tightening as economic activity expands into and through Stage II will probably postpone inflation fears, dampen the rate of increase in interest rates, and prolong the common stock bull market. Stage II tightening may also prevent or mitigate the necessity of a severe monetary restraint in the latter part of Stage III or early Stage IV, which has historically induced a credit crunch.

Fed-created liquidity is not always a cause of rising common stock prices. A loosening Fed policy may depress common stock prices. A tightening Fed policy may boost common stock prices. The reaction of common stock prices depends on where financial markets are in the economic/stock price cycle.

What types of asset allocation tactics can be used?

ACTIVE ASSET ALLOCATION

Active asset allocation requires subjective interpretation of the economic cycle by investors. The investor or portfolio manager must interpret the often confusing and contradictory economic and financial indicators to decide where the financial markets are in the economic/stock price cycle. The emphasis among common stocks, long-term U.S. Treasury bonds, and money market securities shifts accordingly. Ideally, common stocks are bought at their low, switched at their high to money market securities or short positions, and then switched into long term U.S. Treasury bonds or short common stock positions shortly after the peak in economic activity as depicted in Figure 3.1.

PASSIVE ASSET ALLOCATION

The most passive asset allocation approach is buy/hold. Investors continually commit to a well-diversified portfolio of only common stocks at any point on the economic/stock price cycle. The portfolio remains fully committed to common stocks throughout the cycle. The portfolio value fluctuates. Its value is down in bear markets and up in bull markets. The location on the economic/stock price cycle where the common shares were bought varies. The portfolio could be bought at the cyclical high in common stock prices. As long as each succeeding high in common stock prices is higher than the previous high, the portfolio value eventually rises. Even if the common stocks were bought at the prior high, the portfolio value is worth more at the most recent high.

Recent decades of successively higher highs in common stock prices reflect the tendency of the expected earnings numerator in the Equation (3) valuation framework to compound, while interest rates in the denominator remain within a relatively tight range. Occasional spikes and dips in interest rates have depressed or rallied common stock prices. However, for the most part, U.S. long-term interest rates have been stable and relatively low. Thus while the denominator in the Equation (3) valuation framework is relatively stable, the expected earnings numerator compounds over the long term. Common stock prices have a long-term bias to rise if the underlying economy continues to grow, accompanied by rising expected earnings and stable interest rates.

Bear markets have, since the end of World War II, been relatively short compared to bull markets over the economic/stock price cycle. Successive common stock price cycle highs have been higher. The combination of these two patterns has produced relatively high returns to the buy/hold approach. No matter where in the cycle the common stock portfolio had been bought, its value was subsequently higher at the common stock price high in the next cycle.

Dollar Cost Averaging

A variation on the buy/hold of a well-diversified portfolio of common stocks is a rigid, dollar cost averaging purchase of common stocks throughout the cycle. A consistent, constant dollar and periodic purchase of common stocks throughout the cycle reduces the average cost per share in long-run, upward-trending markets. The portfolio return is greater than from a one-time portfolio purchase anywhere in a particular cycle except near the common stock price lows. Over several successively higher highs, the portfolio value increases like its buy/hold cousin.

Constant Percentage Averaging

A further variation on the passive asset allocation approach is the constant percentage, periodic portfolio revision over the economic/ stock price cycle. The common stock portfolio starts at any approximate midpoint in the common stock bull market. Each time a specified, constant percentage rise in common stock prices is reached, a fixed percentage of the portfolio is shifted from stocks into money market securities as the stock price cycle progresses from its low to its high. None of the portfolio is reallocated to long-term U.S. Treasury bonds because interest rates are rising and bond prices falling, in contrast to the rising common stock prices throughout Stages I and II. The cash from the stock sales must be reallocated to the stable value, money market securities. As common stock prices continue to climb toward their current cycle high, more of the portfolio is allocated to money market securities. Eventually almost the entire portfolio is allocated to money market securities, ideally at the high in common stock prices.

The reverse, constant percentage asset reallocation procedure is followed as common stock prices decline through Stages III and IV. A specific portion of the money market securities is sold each time there is a predetermined percentage rise in long-term bond prices, starting shortly after the peak in economic activity in Figure 3.1. Those funds are reallocated to long-term U.S. Treasury bonds to capture their price appreciation as interest rates fall throughout the recession, as depicted in Stages IV in Figure 3.1.

Almost the entire portfolio is allocated to long-term U.S. Treasury bonds at the low in common stock prices. At that point a portion of the long-term bonds is sold and invested in common stocks, ideally at their lows. As the common stock bull market progresses, further portions of the long-term bonds are sold and the funds reallocated to common stocks. The reallocation to common stocks should occur relatively quickly near their lows to capture the majority of the bull market while fully invested in common stocks. A larger proportional reallocation to common stocks would have historically yielded a higher return because bull markets tend to last longer than bear markets.

After the portfolio is fully invested in common stocks and as common stock prices continue to rise during the remainder of their bull market, the portfolio is again reallocated to money market securities. A smaller proportional reallocation is historically preferred because the length of the typical common stock bull market is greater than that of the typical common stock bear market. This constant percentage variation of passive portfolio asset allocation repeats throughout the economic/stock price cycles.

Sector Rotation

The common stock prices of different industries (sectors) respond differently at various points within each of the four Stages of the economic/stock price cycle as depicted in Figure 3.1. "Sector rotation," an active portfolio asset allocation tactic, attempts to capture superior returns by shifting from lower return sectors to higher return sectors as the rotation unfolds.

Common stock prices of interest-rate-sensitive, large-ticket, consumer-durable companies increase first and most rapidly as the stock market passes the low in common stock prices and the shortly following trough in economic activity. The pent-up demand for consumer-durable items, such as housing and cars, has reached it zenith. Consumers had postponed purchasing new houses or new cars during the recession. Families had probably grown and outgrown their apartments. The old car is probably on its last legs and repair bills are more frequent and mounting. The recession-induced lack of confidence and job-loss fear had forced greater savings.

Consumer lack of confidence begins to mitigate as the decline in the recession slows. Consumers may sense economic recovery. Pressures to purchase mount. The restraints on consumer spending break. The time to buy the house and the car is now. Interest rates are low. Mortgage and car payments are affordable. The expected earnings of homebuilders jump from their slump. House prices stabilize. Still, the pent-up demand for housing cannot be satisfied. The same circumstances occur for cars. The expected earnings in the numerator of the Equation (3) valuation framework speed ahead, putting upward pressure on common stock prices of homebuilders and automobile manufacturers. At the same time interest rates continue to fall slightly or remain low and stable. The denominator of the Equation (3) valuation framework has not risen. The combination of rapidly rising expected earnings for homebuilders and auto manufacturers and no downward pressure from interest rates forces the common stock prices of these sectors to rise sharply. The increases in their common stock prices are the largest and most rapid they experience over the economic/stock price cycle. This reflects combination 2 from Table 1.1.

The economic/stock price cycle progresses. Pent-up demand dissipates and interest rates rise slightly. Expected earnings growth slows for the auto and homebuilding sectors. Their common stock price appreciation prospects diminish. Sector rotation allocation investors sell their homebuilding and auto stocks and reallocate into the sectors that are next anticipated to have the greatest acceleration in expected earnings and rising stock prices.

The next most promising sectors in the rotation, as judged by their anticipated increase in expected earnings, are those with relatively high fixed costs that have been minimized during the efficiency efforts of the last recession. The prices of the goods and services sold by these companies have firmed because economic activity and product demand is now expanding. Sectors with the best common stock price appreciation prospects in the middle of Stage II in Figure 3.1 are usually commodity-oriented industries. Examples would be oil producers, refiners, gasoline retailers, steel, aluminum, and other metals producers, and airlines. The largest contribution margins for these sectors are usually observed at this location in the economic/stock price cycle. Their costs are relatively fixed and at cycle lows while demand and prices for their products are firming. Their expected earnings in the numerator of the Equation (3) valuation framework are rising the most rapidly relative to other sectors, such as homebuilders, whose expected earning growth has slowed.

Sector investors now reallocate into the next sectors anticipated to respond with a spurt in expected earnings as the markets progress through the last part of Stage II and into Stage III. The expected earnings growth of the commodity-oriented common stocks slows because of increased production costs, lower efficiency from hiring and training new employees, etc. Sector rotation investors sell commodity-oriented common stocks and buy the next most promising sectors.

The economy is booming. Disposable personal income is high. Common stock prices are high and rising. Consumers feel wealthy and spend more. Luxury item producers and retailers enjoy a renaissance in demand. Cruises and diamonds sell well. More leisure time is demanded and received. The expected earnings of these sectors rise most rapidly toward the end of Stage II and in Stage III. Their expected earnings in the numerator of the Equation (3) valuation framework rise relatively more rapidly than those of other sectors. Their expected earnings outpace the now rapidly rising interest rates in the denominator of the Equation (3) valuation framework. Their common stock prices rise while the other sectors with less rapidly rising expected earnings growth flatten or fall.

The capital goods sectors experience their most rapid and significant expected earnings increase in Stage III. The overcapacity experienced by their customers during the prior recession and carried through the early and middle parts of Stage II no longer exists. Manufacturers now, almost in unison, turn to capital goods producers and plant and equipment providers. Production capacity must be expanded. Orders for capital goods are backlogged. Prices for capital goods rise. Capital goods producers expected earnings in the numerator of the Equation (3) valuation framework experience a greater rate of increase than the now rapidly rising interest rates in the denominator of the Equation (3) valuation framework. Their common stock prices rise.

Sector allocation investors rarely find outperforming industries during the relatively short, last part of Stage III. Interest rates typically rise so rapidly that expected earnings of most firms cannot keep up. Common stock prices fall. Only short sellers profit. Gloom pervades most other investors, who are long and must wait until the dawn of Stage IV to find industry sectors that will outperform general market averages.

Stage IV witnesses declining common stock prices and falling long-term U.S. Treasury bond yields (higher prices). Common stock prices decline because expected earnings decline at a faster rate than interest rates decline. High-quality, long-term bond prices are rising because interest rates are falling in the recession.

The expected earnings of certain sectors are less affected by the recession than others. The expected earnings in those sectors fall at a slower rate of decrease than the rate of decrease in interest rates. The expected earnings in the numerator of the Equation (3) valuation framework for these sectors fall more slowly than the rate of decrease in interest rates in the denominator. The common stock prices of these sectors rise while the rest of the stock market falls. The expected earnings of other sectors may be countercyclical and remain stable or grow, furthering their relatively superior sector return.

Common stocks most likely to show superior returns relative to the general stock market during Stage IV are labeled "defensive." Most of these firms have expected earnings that are resistant to the negative effects of the recession. Their earnings environments are noted for the necessity and income inelasticity of their product or service. Prominent examples include residential electrical and gas utilities, food producers and retailers, and pharmaceutical companies. These are necessities that consumers must have regardless of the recession and its negative impact on their incomes. Sector rotation investors envision moderately declining, stable, or moderately rising earnings for these firms. In the first situation the expected earnings in the numerator of the Equation (3) valuation framework are declining at a lower rate of decrease than the rate of decrease in interest rates in the denominator. In the other two situations expected earnings are steady or modestly rising while interest rates in the denominator are falling. These situations reflect combinations 9b, 3, or 2, respectively, of Table 1.1. The common stock prices of these defensive issues rise during Stage IV.

SUMMARY

Active asset allocation should emphasize different proportions of common stocks, money market securities, and long-term U.S. Treasury bonds in different Stages of the economic/stock price cycle.

Stage I asset allocation should emphasize common stocks. Expected earnings are usually rising at their fastest rate over the economic/stock price cycle and at a much faster rate of increase than interest rates. Common stock prices rise throughout Stage I as a result.

Stage II asset allocation should continue to emphasize common stocks. The rate of increase in expected earnings, albeit slower than in Stage I, remains greater than the rate of increase in interest rates. Common stock prices continue to rise.

Stage III asset allocation should emphasize money market securities. Interest rates rise most rapidly in Stage III. The rate of increase in interest rates overtakes the now slower rate of increase in expected earnings. Common stock prices *and* long-term bond prices tend to fall most precipitously in Stage III. Money market securities and short positions are the only asset categories with positive returns in Stage III.

Stage IV asset allocation should emphasize long-term U.S. Treasury bonds. This Stage is associated with recessions. Interest rates decline and high-quality bond prices rise in recessions. In this Stage, expected earnings for most firms fall faster than interest rates. Common stock prices decline. Asset allocations in long-term, high-quality bonds or short sales and defensive common stocks garner capital gains.

Sector rotation should emphasize different industry sectors in different Stages of the economic/stock price cycle, depending on the relative rate of increase in expected earnings for that sector in that Stage.

Stage I sectors with relatively superior, near-term earnings respond to the combined stimuli of low interest rates, recovering consumer confidence, and released pent-up consumer demand for high-priced consumer durables, such as cars and houses. The common stock prices of these sectors respond first and faster than other sectors. However, their relatively superior return performance fades as the financial markets progress through the economic/stock price cycle.

Stage II sectors with a relatively superior rate of earnings growth differ from those in Stage I. Early in Stage II, firming commodity prices increase the earnings of natural resource firms, such as oil and metals producers, as well as certain service industries, such as airlines. Many of these sectors have relatively fixed cost structures. They are also operating at their most efficient point in the economic/stock price cycle, a legacy from recession cost-cutting efforts. Their fixed-cost structure and high-operating efficiency propel the rate of increase in their earnings expectations to their highest level in the economic/stock price cycle.

In Stage III, economic expansion booms, inflation accelerates, confidence grows, personal income reaches new heights, and production capacity strains. Sector rotation investors envision relatively superior expected earnings growth in different industries than those in Stage I and Stage II. The expected earnings of luxury-item producers, retailers, and capital-goods producers, for example, rise at a faster rate than the rate of increase in interest rates. The common stock prices of these and similar industry sectors rise relatively more rapidly than

the flattening or declining general stock market. As the economic/
stock price cycle enters Stage IV and the economy rolls over into
recession, the relatively superior earnings growth of these sectors
fades. Their stock prices relatively underperform.

Stage IV experiences different impacts of the recession on the expected earnings of different sectors. The defensive industries, for
which sector rotation investors anticipate slowly increasing, stable, or
moderately declining earnings through the recession, are emphasized.
Their relatively superior earnings performance, coupled with declining interest rates, generates relatively superior common stock price
performance.

NOTE

1. The ripple effects of the original OPEC (The Organization of Petro-
leum Exporting Countries) price shock took almost a decade to unwind.
More recent, albeit milder, oil price swings, some caused by OPEC, continue
to strike and ripple throughout the economic/stock price cycle.

Appendix 4A

Sector Rotation Categories

STAGE I
Autos
Containers
Railroads
Trucking
Housing
Furniture/Appliances

STAGE II
Apparel
Broadcasting
Office Supplies
Retail

Construction

Stock Brokers/Investment Bankers

Hotels

STAGE III

Real Estate

Capital Equipment/Machinery

Travel

Airlines

Commercial Aircraft

Steel

Metals

Motion Pictures

Publishing

Jewelry

Banking

Insurance

Cosmetics/Toiletries

Office Equipment

Printing

Paper

Oil

STAGE IV

Electrical Utilities

Other Utilities

Funeral Services

Food

Soap Household Products

Telephone

Beverages

Cable TV

Medical
Pharmaceuticals
Defense
Tobacco

5

Individual Stock Price
Implications

*Are there valuation implications for individual common stocks
within the Equation (3) valuation framework?*

Of course there are. Specific risks applicable to each company and its
common stock must be considered in its valuation. These risks are
distinct from and in addition to the general market risks, identified
in prior chapters as fluctuations in expected earnings growth, real
interest rates, and inflation. Company-specific risks can be mitigated
through diversification. General market risks cannot.

An appropriately diversified portfolio of common stocks can mitigate the risks of separate, individually-owned common stocks. Common stocks within a portfolio may respond differently from the same
event. For example, an increase in oil prices may increase the expected
earnings for oil companies while simultaneously decreasing the expected earnings for airlines. Investors owning only airline common
stocks lose. Investors owning only oil common stocks gain. Investors
owning both oil and airline common stocks experience an offsetting
effect. Their portfolios garner the average return. The portfolio return is not as large as it would have been if solely invested in oil and
not as small as it would have been if solely invested in airlines. The
portfolio risk has been reduced without a corresponding decrease in
the average return. A completely diversified portfolio including every
common stock eliminates all company-specific risks but always retains
general common stock market risks.

Little risk mitigation comes from owning an individual common stock or sector that responds to the same underlying expected earnings and risk factors. For example, a portfolio of two U.S. car manufacturers or several major, domestic U.S. airlines has very little risk mitigation from diversification. Investors must analyze the specific risks associated with an individual common stock or industry sector.

Portfolio concentration increases the possible return as well as the risk. As concentration increases, company-specific risks are more pronounced. As diversification increases, company-specific risks are mitigated. General common stock market risks can never be eliminated or reduced unless combined with other categories of assets, such as money market funds and bonds.

What categories of specific risks must investors in individual common stocks identify?

Categories of specific risks can be identified. Investors should focus on these categories and be alert for changes. Changes in any identified category cause changes in the valuation. Investors must incorporate these specific risk categories into the Equation (3) valuation framework for individual common stocks.

Investors' valuation of individual common stocks, unlike that of a well-diversified portfolio, must recognize increased risk by adding a required return in the denominator of the Equation (3) valuation framework. In effect the risk is "built-up" in the denominator as each category of specific risk is included. Financial jargon frequently refers to the resulting valuation framework as the "build-up" model. The risk build-up of the denominator in the Equation (3) valuation framework reconfigures it from:

$$P = \Sigma_{t = 1, \infty} E_t(1 - \Lambda)/(1 + r)^t \qquad\qquad (3)$$

to:

$$P = \Sigma_{t = 1, \infty} E_t(1 - \Lambda) / (1 + i + p + e + s + b + f + m + o)^t$$

where:

P   = common stock price

$\Sigma_{t=1, \infty}$ = the sum of the future from now to infinity

E_t = the expected earnings in each future year t

Λ = the percentage of expected earnings (E) retained. $1 - \Lambda$
                is the payout rate

The nondiversifiable, general market risk components that combine to form the general equity market risk associated with receiving the expected earnings in the numerator are as follows:

i   = the real interest rate risk

p   = purchasing power risk premium, reflecting inflation expectations

e   = general equity risk premium

Common stocks are fungible and compete with U.S. Treasury bonds, the default-risk-free alternative. However, common stocks can never be as default risk free as U.S. Treasury securities, since companies cannot print legal tender at will. The expected earnings of a common stock may not be realized. The contractual interest payments and return of principal on U.S. Treasury bonds will certainly be realized.

A risk gap between common stocks and U.S. Treasury bonds always exists. Investors require an additional return above the U.S. Treasury bond yield (i + p) from common stocks. This gap cannot be diversified away in a portfolio of common stocks; it can only be mitigated when U.S. Treasury bonds are folded into a portfolio of common stocks. The additional, general equity risk premium (e) in the denominator of the Equation (3) valuation framework increases the required rate of return for common stocks over that of the U.S. Treasury bond yield (i + p). This equity risk premium has been chronicled extensively. The Ibbotson studies, for example, measure the general equity risk premium as relatively stable over the long horizon within substantial annual fluctuations.

The specific risks built on the general equity market risks (i + p

+ e) to reflect the additional risks of receiving company expected earnings in the Equation (3) valuation framework above or below the average equity risk premium are:

s   = size

b   = business (operating) risk inherent in the industry or company operating environment

f   = the company degree of financial leverage (use of debt to finance assets)

m   = the marketability of the common stock as measured by the number of shares that can be sold or bought without destabilizing the current share price (sometimes referred to as liquidity)

o   = other risks that may materialize from sources outside the specific risk categories already identified.

The required rate of return (r) in the Equation (3) valuation framework for individual common stocks is as follows: r = the required rate of return used to discount the future expected earnings. It is the sum of the general equity market risks that can *not* be mitigated through diversification *plus* the individual company risks that can be mitigated through diversification.

SIZE

The Ibbotson studies document a higher required rate of return for smaller companies that varies inversely with size. Some companies have been "too large to fail." The U.S. government has rescued large banks, other types of financial institutions, and Chrysler. Smaller firms are rarely, if ever, rescued. Size, like the other company-specific risks, may be reduced through diversification. A portfolio that includes every common stock averages firm sizes and the associated risk.

BUSINESS RISK

Business risk (b), also known as operating risk, evolves from the underlying characteristics of the business and its operating environment. Every business has its own set of operating circumstances that can change and, in turn, cause changes in expected earnings. Higher

levels of business risk are typically associated with more cyclical industries and any company with expected earnings more difficult to
forecast consistently and accurately. As business risk increases, the
denominator in the Equation (3) valuation framework also increases,
implying a greater return to compensate for the heightened risk. The
common stock price, in effect the present value of the expected earnings, is lower.

A change in business risk changes, in turn, the common stock price.
An increase in business risk for the expected earnings reduces the
common stock price. A decrease in business risk for the expected
earnings increases the common stock price.

The common stock price changes in response to a change in business risk even if the expected earnings remain the same. A change in
business risk implies that the probability of the company actually
achieving expected earnings has changed, not that the expected earnings have actually changed. There is a higher or lower probability
expected earnings would be realized. Business risk in the denominator
of the Equation (3) valuation framework has changed, and in turn,
the present value of the expected earnings has changed.

Reported earnings that differ from expected earnings change the
common stock price. At a constant level of risk in the denominator
of the Equation (3) valuation framework, differences in the reported
earnings below the expected earnings change common stock prices.
A shortfall in reported earnings from expected earnings typically decreases common stock prices. Conversely, reported earnings above
the expected earnings typically increase the common stock price.
These reported deviations from expected earnings cause common
stock price changes to occur even if the risk associated with achieving
future expected earnings remains unchanged.

Specific risks are extensive and far-ranging over industries and
companies. The investor must examine each individual company's operating environment and determine the specific risks that are present.
Electrical utilities and other defensive stocks usually have a higher
degree of certainty associated with their expected earnings and con-
sequently have less risk of reported earnings deviating from expected
earnings. For example, less business risk (b) is built into the electrical
utilities common stock required rate of return. The denominator in
the Equation (3) valuation framework is smaller relative to other industries with more uncertainty in their expected earnings, such as
"aggressive growth" and cyclical common stocks.

Companies in industries with significant competition and no or few barriers to entry usually are considered high business risks. The home-shopping craze witnessed spectacular early success for the first entrant. Its rapid earnings growth prospects were crushed when hordes of competitors soon entered. The availability of inexpensive television time and merchandise lured many competitive attempts to cash in on the spectacular growth of the originator. Market saturation quickly killed not only the originator's growth but also the expected earnings of all participants. Home-shopping stocks crumbled. The "shakeout" of the marginal operators left only a few strong firms with much reduced earnings growth prospects and common stock prices.

Companies can change their business risk to varying degrees. Sometimes the operating characteristics underlying the business are controllable. Other times operating characteristics are not controllable. Dell Computer, the successful direct seller of personal computers, changed the industry's traditional inventory cycle and business risk of obsolescence by almost entirely eliminating inventory. Dell builds personal computers from just-in-time inventory parts and only after the product has been sold. There is little inventory to store or to obsolesce. Expected earnings can be forecasted with increased certainty. Business risk is lower. The Dell common stock price valuation is higher for the expected earnings. Yet, even Dell experienced supply chain disruptions when the 1999 Taiwan earthquake hit its suppliers. Earthquakes generally fall under the "other" risk category.

Operating characteristics are often hard to change. For example, businesses that operate solely in a politically-unstable environment and cannot diversify or shift to more stable environments have higher business risk and lower common stock price valuations for the expected earnings. The common stocks of corporations operating in Russia during the late 1990s had large business risk because of the political uncertainty under which they operated. Their valuations were lower. When the risk of political instability materialized, their expected earnings and common stock prices collapsed. Companies operating in Russia during this time could do little to change their business risk.

Companies with high embedded fixed costs have more frequent and larger fluctuations in their expected earnings. Their operating leverage makes expected earnings of these firms more cyclical. These companies are less capable of adjusting costs to compensate for falling revenues. Conversely, their costs do not rise proportionately with revenues. Large hard-to-forecast fluctuations in expected earnings occur. Earnings forecasting is relatively more difficult. Business risk is higher. The common stock price for the expected earnings is lower. The steel industry is an example. Uncontrollable changes of a few pennies in the foreign exchange rate with a competing, steel-producing nation cause significant changes in the expected earnings of domestic steel producers.

The ability and inability of OPEC to raise or lower oil prices affects the expected earnings of oil producers. Yet these producers have no direct control over OPEC. Their associated business risk is higher and their common stock prices lower for the expected earnings. Oil producers must take controllable, offsetting actions to reduce the uncontrollable OPEC business risk. These actions can range from clever futures hedging to cost-cutting efficiencies.

A change in management may also reduce business risk. Better management likely makes better business decisions. Business risk is reduced. Common stock prices rise for the expected earnings. If expected earnings also increase, the common stock price rises more.

A company-perceived business risk attracts different types of stockholders or investor clientele. More risk-averse investors favor common stocks of firms with a higher degree of certainty in expected earnings, in other words less business risk. Less risk-averse investors favor common stocks of firms with a lower degree of certainty in expected earnings but anticipated higher returns.

Conglomerates, operating across many different environments with different degrees of business risk, have reacted to the investor clientele by separating different operating environments into less and more risky firms. The more certain expected earnings of the less risky firm have a higher value for its expected earnings. The associated business risk has decreased. More risk-averse investors now buy the expected earnings at a higher valuation. Simultaneously the expected earnings growth of the higher business risk firm is more obvious. That firm is also valued more highly because that growth is no longer dragged down by the less rapidly growing segments of the conglomerate. Less risk-averse investors value the new firm's stock more highly because the expected earnings growth in the numerator of the Equation (3) valuation framework has increased more than the increase in the business risk of the new firm.

Firms sometimes use "tracking stocks" to appeal to different investor clienteles and to enhance total value. Different segments of the firm with different degrees of certainty attached to expected earnings and risks are tracked separately. Usually, separate dividend-oriented and capital-gains-oriented tracking stocks are created to appeal to different clienteles. Total value may be increased since each investor clientele pays more for the expected earnings from each tracking stock. The sum of the two tracking stocks' valuations is more than the previous valuation of the single stock of the whole firm. Companies using tracking stocks include AT&T and General Motors.

FINANCIAL RISK

Financial risk (f) in the Equation (3) valuation framework is controlled by the firm. The decision to borrow or not to borrow is usually carefully analyzed. Management is typically not forced to borrow, which in more technical financial jargon is called "leverage." The degree to which firms leverage is to a great extent a function of the degree to which management is more or less averse to borrowing and, sometimes, the willingness of lenders to lend. Firms' leveraging decisions signal valuation implications to investors.

An over-leveraged or under-leveraged position affects the common stock price. The over-leveraged firm, as judged by investors, increases its financial risk. Leverage increases the potential volatility of expected earnings and the difficulty of forecasting them. The probability also increases that the firm may not meet its debt service obligations on a timely basis in an internal cash flow slowdown.

The financial risk component in the denominator of the Equation (3) valuation framework increases as the degree of financial leverage increases. The common stock price must decline for the expected earnings. The negative impact on the common stock price accelerates after the firm exceeds an acceptable leverage threshold. This negative impact accelerates further as the degree of over-leverage increases. Investors may tolerate a little over-leverage if the prospects are that the firm will decrease to a more acceptable, "normal leverage" by repaying some of the borrowing or growing equity. Investors rarely tolerate over-leverage without penalizing the common stock price.

Loan repayment schedules also affect the degree of financial risk. Large balloon (bullet) payments heighten the possibility of default or disadvantageous refinancing. The degree of financial risk increases in these situations as time to repayment shortens. Investors must be alert to impending large repayment deadlines and reflect this in their common stock valuations.

Leveraged buyouts (LBO) are examples of extreme leverage. Buyers almost completely replace equity with debt. The common stock price of the remaining equity falls dramatically, sometimes to pennies. The buyers envision repaying the debt from the expected cash flow of the bought company. As the debt is repaid, more of the company value returns to the common stock. The common stock price rises. This is analogous to buying a home with little money down. The house is used as collateral to secure the large loan. The gradual repayment of the mortgage shifts more of the home value into the homeowner's equity. The eventual repayment of the entire mortgage leaves the homeowner with all the equity. The value of the home need not increase for the homeowner to realize a relatively large gain.

This LBO financial strategy is often applied several times by both investors and homeowners for the same firm or home. The firm is bought with borrowed funds. The borrowings are repaid from the firm's own cash flow. All the equity belongs to the common stock. Common stockholders leverage the firm again, usually withdraw the money, repay the loan from the firm's cash flow, and again eventually shift all the firm's value back to the common stockholders. As long as the firm's cash flow is sufficient to meet the debt service, the process may be repeated. Private firms have been known to sell the firm back to themselves, in effect, several times within one or two generations. Sometimes this provides liquidity for estate planning and diversification opportunities for the stockholders.

Why do firms leverage? The motivation to leverage is explained in the Equation (3) valuation framework. Leverage affects both the numerator and the denominator. If leverage increases expected earnings in the numerator more than it increases financial risk in the denominator, the common stock price rises. This occurs when the operating rate of return on assets exceeds the interest rate paid (the pretax cost of debt capital) without a more than offsetting increase in the financial risk component of the required rate of return (cost of equity) in the denominator of the Equation (3) valuation framework. The rate of return on the assets purchased exceeds the cost of the borrowed funds. This is positive financial leverage. The favorable impact on the per share common stock price is magnified further because fewer shares are sold to finance the assets. Fewer shares divide the increased expected earnings, and expected earnings per share are larger.

Negative financial leverage is the converse. When the operating return on assets is less than the interest rate paid (pretax cost of debt capital) on the borrowings, the common stock price falls. The financial risk in the denominator of the Equation (3) valuation framework increases while the expected earnings in the numerator falls. This is combination 7 from Table 1.1. The negative impact on the per share common stock price is magnified. Of course no firm intentionally tries to achieve negative financial leverage. It just happens.

The common stock price falls if the expected earning rate of increase is not as fast as the rate of increase in financial risk. This reflects combination 8b of Table 1.1. The relatively smaller increase in expected earnings compared to financial risk occurs most often when over-leverage jumps beyond investors' tolerance for additional leverage. Financial risk accelerates rapidly at and above this point. Investors' default and expected earnings forecast difficulties outweigh their envisioned favorable impact on expected earnings. The common stock price falls.

The under-leveraged position may signal that the shareholder wealth maximization effort could be more acute. Failure to grow expected earnings by not employing positive financial leverage causes the common stock price to be less than it otherwise might be. The expected earnings in the numerator of the Equation (3) valuation framework are not as large. The financial risk in the denominator does not increase because no leverage has occurred. Nevertheless the common stock price is lower than it might otherwise be because expected earnings could increase faster than financial risk with the use of leverage. The firm's overall (weighted average) cost of capital is higher. Shareholders wealth is not maximized.

A leveraging of the under-leveraged firm often increases its common stock price even if *total* company expected earnings in the numerator of the Equation (3) valuation framework remain unchanged or decline slightly. The firm borrows money to repurchase some of its shares. If the earnings per share increase proportionately more than financial risk increases, the per share common stock price increases.

How do investors judge what is over-leveraged and under-leveraged? First, the firm must be judged as able to meet its debt service on a timely basis. Investors examine the firm's historical debt service coverage, particularly during its severest earnings decline. Second, the firm must have been able to meet its debt service under the most adverse of cash flow circumstances. Third, the firm must not have increased its debt service burden from the level prevailing under that adverse time. Investors must envision no worse circumstances occurring in the future. If all of the above three judgments converge, investors assign limited financial risk.

Investors also judge a firm's leveraged position in comparison to the historical industry norm leveraged position. The debt/equity and the debt/total capital ratios are measures often used. The common stock price of an over-leveraged firm, by this judgmental standard, sells at a lower price for the expected earnings than an identical firm with an industry norm leverage position.

The leverage buyout of Federated Department Stores during the height of the LBO craze is an example of over-leverage. It caused the common stock price of Federated Department Stores to fall. The sequence of events started in the traditional LBO fashion. Large borrowings financed the acquisition of this conservatively managed and well-established chain of department stores. Debt was ambitiously sought in all forms and from all sources and became an extremely high percentage of the capital structure. The cash-flow-oriented debt service coverage measure, based on earnings before interest, taxes, depreciation, and amortization (EBITDA), was about one. This meant that all internally-generated cash flow had to be used to meet current debt service. There was no room for error. A debt service coverage ratio below one means the firm does not have sufficient internally-generated cash flow to meet its interest and principal payments on a timely basis. Federated Department Stores had no reserve borrowing capacity to meet a cash flow shortfall. All the money that could be borrowed had been borrowed. The firm was extremely over-leveraged. The lenders owned the firm at that point. Equity value was minimal.

The Federated Department Stores LBO hoped that future, internally-generated cash flow would service its debt. With no margin for error, error occurred. A relatively mild recession, which would normally have been survived by Federated Department Stores, slightly reduced total earnings and cash flow. The firm could not meet its debt service and went bankrupt. Components of Federated Department Stores that had survived the Great Depression of the 1930s could not survive a mild recession. Federated Department Stores went bankrupt under the weight of its own over-leverage.

MARKETABILITY RISK

Marketability risk (m), frequently labeled liquidity risk, is the risk of being unable to purchase or sell a given number of shares at the current market price. As the number of shares to be bought or sold increases relative to the current bid or ask size, marketability risk increases. Marketability risk is associated with the shares themselves, unlike business risk that is associated with the firm operations and financial risk that is associated with the firm capital structure. A relatively large block of common stock bought or sold into a small, inactive market causes price changes adverse to the investor. The selling investor must attract additional buyers to purchase the greater than usual number of shares to be sold. Reducing the bid price is the natural and, perhaps, the only way to entice additional buyers to come forth. The common stock price sinks. Market risk has materialized. The reverse occurs for a relatively large buy order. The common stock price rises to entice additional sellers.

Marketability risk is the converse of marketability. As the number of shares that may be bought or sold at the current market price increases, marketability increases but marketability risk decreases. Increases in marketability decrease marketability risk and increase the common stock price for the expected earnings.

Marketability risk is another factor in the denominator of the Equation (3) valuation framework. The common stock price for the expected earnings is inversely related to the degree of marketability risk. A high marketability risk requires a higher rate of return and a lower common stock price for the expected earnings.

When marketability risk materializes for a common stock, that common stock price changes. The same is true for other types of securities. An upward change in marketability risk causes a downward change in the common stock price and vice versa. This is reflected in the Equation (3) valuation framework by an increase or decrease in the denominator and a corresponding decrease or increase, respectively, in the common stock price. Combinations 4 and 3, respectively, from Table 1.1 reflect this change, assuming all other factors in the valuation framework remain unchanged.

The degree of impact from a change in marketability risk varies according to the specific situation. An initial public offering significantly reduces the marketability risk of a specific common stock or other type of security. Dealers or exchange specialists who make markets usually trade the newly-issued common stock. Someone is usually ready to buy or sell the shares. This is distinctly different from the private, nonmarketable status of these shares before the initial public offer.

The initial public offering impact on marketability risk and the common stock price is significant. Publicly-traded common shares rise an average of 40% or more immediately upon becoming public compared to their privately-held value. Looked at in reverse, privately-held common shares are usually valued at a 40% or more discount from identical publicly-traded counterparts. The ability to buy or sell the shares quickly and at the current market price is valuable. This ability and the corporate-management decision to "go public" reduce marketability risk and increase the common stock price. The greatest reduction in marketability risk and, correspondingly, greatest increase in common stock price from that reduction occurs once, upon the initial public offering.

Further management actions to reduce marketability risk (increase marketability) have considerably less impact, although the degree varies among the types of actions taken. A move from bulletin board trading to a national over-the-counter listing, and vice versa, is more substantial in most cases than a move from a national over-the-counter listing to an organized exchange. Once actively traded, exchange listings or further increases in the number of market makers usually add relatively small increments to marketability and small decreases in marketability risk.

Stock splits have similar gradations of impact on marketability risk. Stock splits that significantly increase the number of shareholders or help meet listing requirements affect the common stock price more than stock splits that increase an existing large number of shares and shareholders of an already actively traded common stock. For example, Proctor and Gamble split its shares two-for-one, increasing the number outstanding from about 600 million to 1.2 billion shares. No noticeable stock price response occurred.

Marketability risk is unique to any issue of common stock at any specific time and varies among securities issued by the same firm. Investors, particularly minority position owners, in privately-held companies have almost no marketability associated with their common stock. The lack of an active market for these privately-held shares may be further exacerbated by restrictions on their transfer, frequently observed in family and closely-held corporations. At the other extreme, investors in large publicly-traded corporations with large "float" (freely traded shares) have high marketability and little marketability risk.

Relatively high marketability diminishes when a significant number of shares relative to the total outstanding shares is closely held. A large holding relative to the float affects marketability and its mirror image, marketability risk.

Investors often observe a shift in marketability in secondary distributions and tender offers. Relatively large secondary distributions often force shares below recent small-lot share prices to elicit enough demand to absorb the shares offered. In effect this is moving down the demand curve in the typical supply/demand curve configuration. Conversely, tenders for relatively large blocks of shares usually force the price above recent small-lot prices. The tender must offer this higher price to draw out a greater supply of shares at this moment. In effect the tender is moving up the supply curve. Part of the price increase associated with the tender may reflect a control premium if control is involved.

Time mitigates marketability risk. A relatively large block of shares can be bought or sold with less impact on the current share price if executed in smaller increments over time. Large block investors can control the marketability risk and its price impact to some degree by spreading their shares sales or purchases over time. However, other factors may change within that time span and mitigate or offset the envisioned reduction in marketability risk.

Marketability risk is specific to different securities issued by the same corporation. Investors frequently observe varying degrees of marketability risk among the bonds, common shares, and preferred shares of the same issuer. The common stock may have a relatively large float and trade in large volume within a tight bid/ask spread and with small price changes. The preferred stock or bonds of the same issuer may have a relatively small float and trade in small volume within a wide bid/ask spread and large price changes. Preferred stocks sometimes trade in very small lots but experience wide price swings on trades of a few shares. The direction of the price swing, of course, depends on whether the shares are sold or bought. There is no market continuity and extremely little float. Investors who want to buy or sell these shares must pay the price to elicit a response from the other side of the market.

Marketability risk can be envisioned in terms of the Equation (3) valuation framework. The current common stock price reflects the specific situation marketability risk at current expected earnings and other risks. Any change in marketability risk changes (m) in the denominator. A decrease in marketability risk increases the common stock price for the expected earnings. Conversely, an increase in marketability risk decreases the common stock price for the expected earnings.

OTHER RISKS

The future is fraught with risks beyond those categorized to this point. Investors simply cannot see the future with accuracy, as hard as they try. Risks materialize where investors would never think. Seemingly defensive corporations, such as food retailers, are accused of selling tainted meat. Embezzlements and accounting irregularities appear as if from nowhere, even among well-respected firms. There is no tendency for one particular type of firm to be more prone to these unusual occurrences. Investors cannot identify or logically incorporate these "other" risks into any valuation framework. These risks lurk in the shadows and randomly appear to the bane of investors.

SUMMARY

Categories of company-specific risks exist beyond the general market risks of changes in interest rates, inflation, equity risk premium, and unrealized expected earnings. Individual company's exposure to these risks varies and is often beyond management control. Changes in these risks affect common stock prices.

Size

Size affects risk. Larger companies tend to be less risky. The largest companies may be too large to fail and are supported by a government safety net.

Business Risk

The company's operating environment creates risk. Volatile environments create higher risk. Earnings fluctuate more and are harder to predict. The common stock price is lower for the expected earnings. Company management often cannot control the operating environment that encompasses a broad range of factors, such as government regulation, political climates, business cycle sensitivity, etc. A decrease in business risk exerts upward pressure on the individual company common stock price. An increase in business risk puts downward pressure on the common stock price for the expected earnings.

Financial Risk

The degree to which a company uses debt affects the risk associated with the common stock price. Earnings volatility increases as the proportion of debt used to finance the company increases. Uncertainty, beyond that already associated with the realization of expected earnings, accompanies debt. Yet companies use debt because of its lower cost of capital and potential for positive financial leverage and favorable impact on their common stock prices.

Marketability Risk

Investors risk affecting the common stock price by buying or selling a number of shares beyond the currently quoted market size. The purchase or sale of such a number of shares at one time may cause the common stock price to fluctuate against the investor. The sale or purchase of large blocks often moves the common stock price. Bids are often well above the current minority position common stock price when all the shares of a company are bought at one time.

Other Risks

All risks do not fit conveniently in the enumerated categories. Investors cannot possibly foresee all risks. Unidentified or undiscovered risks are categorized as "other." Investors know they lurk out there. A surprise change in other risks affects the prevailing common stock price.

6

Industry Life Cycle

Does the company's stage in its industry life cycle affect its common stock price?

Investors label common stocks and industries according to the pattern of their expected earnings. The major categories are venture capital, growth, mature, and stable/declining. Corporations and industries within these categories usually progress through the various categories, from "birth to death." This trek is the industry life cycle.

INDUSTRY LIFE CYCLE

The dynamic forces of a capitalist economy naturally create significant changes in the expected earnings and risk environments for corporations. New ideas come forth and develop. Unique, superior profit opportunities emerge, only to be withered away by imitating competitors. Superior profits turn average. Further new ideas come forth, develop, and turn average profits into declining profits. Entire industries disappear. The economy goes on. The birth to death life cycle repeats with different players.

These dynamics are illustrated in Figure 6.1, the industry life cycle. The venture capital stage is most closely associated with the new ideas, the visions, and the aspirations yet to be attained. The rapid growth stage emerges as the vision turns to implementation. The euphoria surrounding the first success fosters rapid growth and com-

Figure 6.1
Industry Life Cycle

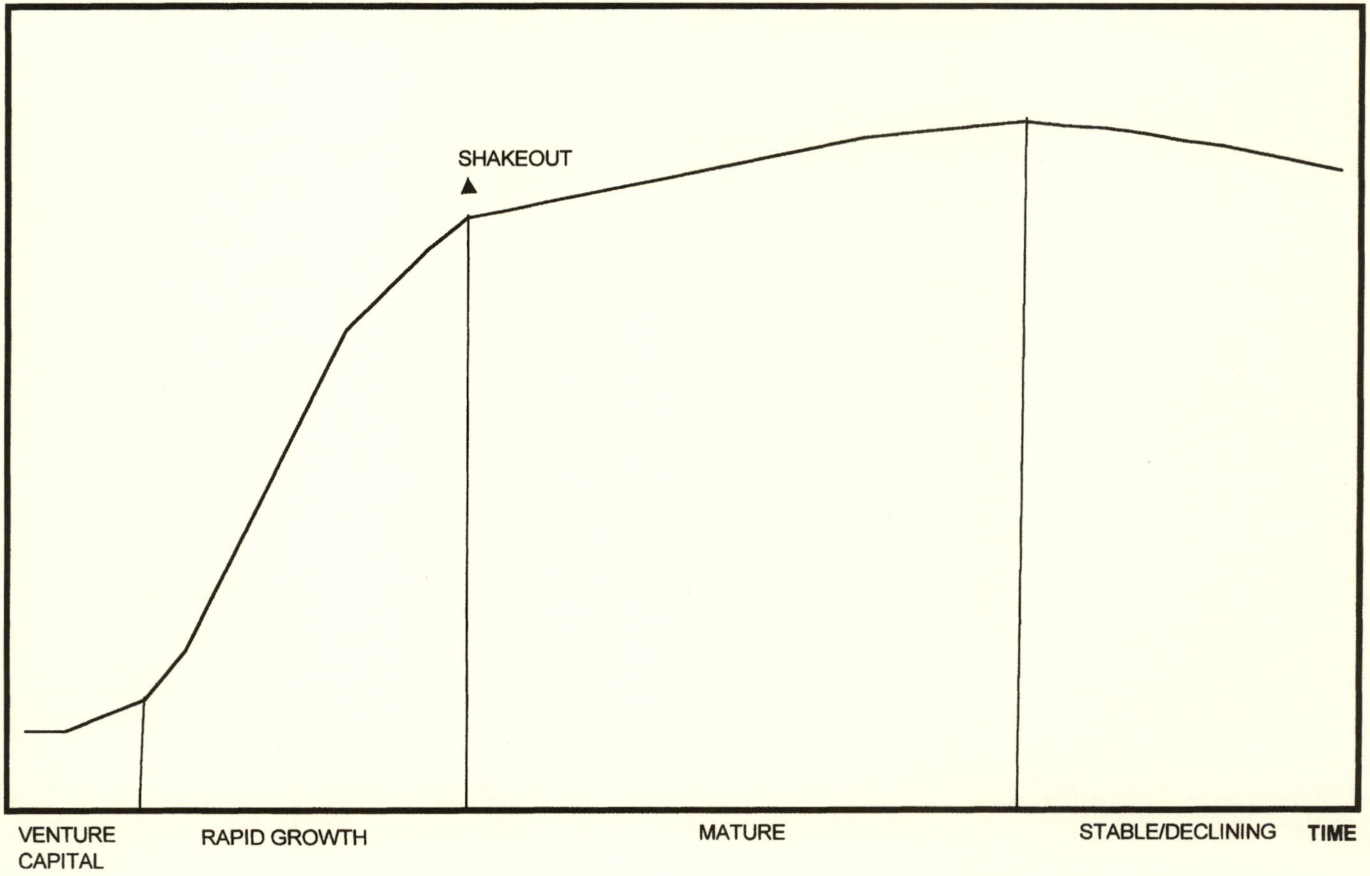

VENTURE CAPITAL | RAPID GROWTH | SHAKEOUT | MATURE | STABLE/DECLINING | TIME

petition that ends in a shakeout of marginal players. The mature stage survivors entrench into the economic mainstream. Many become "blue chips." Yet they are not immune to the competitive dynamics. Unless they reinvent themselves, they sink into the stable/declining stage, pushed by new venture capital stage companies.

The duration of the trek through the life cycle varies among industries and companies. Woolworth, for example, operated over a century and still clings on as a shadow of its former self. The five-and-dime retail store concept was held in little regard when first introduced. Woolworth could find little financial backing and failed several times. Despite this the Woolworth store became a ubiquitous feature on the retail landscape. Its common stock was among the blue chips listed in the Dow Jones Industrial Average. Eventually, however, newer trends in retailing, such as discount and specialty stores, emerged. Woolworth languished. Its five-and-dime variety stores as well as its name disappeared. Its common stock was dropped from the Dow Jones Industrial Average. Its name vanished in the United States as it became Venator, a shadow of its former self in the guise of specialty footwear stores. Woolworth's life cycle lasted over a century. Some industry life cycles that started over a century ago continue. Other life cycles have been much shorter.

VENTURE CAPITAL STAGE

Newly-born industries, such as the Internet, are nurtured through their formative years as speculative venture capital situations with all their value and expected earnings nothing more than investors' vision of benefits to come. The entire corporation may be no more than an idea, a vision, or sketch of an entrepreneur who has been funded. The corporate headquarters may be no more than a garage, as at the birth of Apple Computer.

The basic premise is to combine funds with the entrepreneur's idea to spark and energize the initial steps in the life cycle. The venture capital investor must look not only at the idea but also at the entrepreneur. The investment is as much in the entrepreneur as in the idea. Investors expect the entrepreneur's full devotion to the corporation, much like a doting father or mother would give a newborn child. Investors must have an appropriate appreciation of the required funding and a willingness to commit. Most venture capital investments are nonmarketable, and commitment is inescapable.

The investment analysis of venture capital common stock is complex yet simple in concept. The only two areas available to be analyzed are the probability of the idea selling profitably and the entrepreneurial management skills. No operating or financial track record exists. Business plan projections may or may not be solidly grounded in sound logic or foresight. Investors must check their vision and judgments against those in the business plan as a basis for investment decisions.

The valuation of the venture capital common stock remains grounded in the concept of the present value of envisioned, distant, large earnings discounted back to the present by a high required rate of return. The guidance of the Equation (3) valuation framework remains but is considerably less precise. The expected earnings in the numerator are negative until some distant year in which breakeven, succeeded by rapid earnings growth, emerges. Those anticipated large earnings, even though discounted at a high required rate of return to compensate for the high risk, give current value to the common stock. The annual required rate of return in the denominator of the Equation (3) valuation framework often exceeds 50%. A portion of this high required rate of return is caused by the nonmarketability of the shares. Another portion is caused by the other, obvious major business and finance risks.

The common stock price usually remains relatively low during the venture capital years of development and losses. Suddenly, with the realization that this particular corporation has successfully trekked through the venture capital stage, previously distant revenues and profits are more easily envisioned and perhaps quantified. The dormant stock price awakes from hibernation and scrambles upwards. Venture capital investors envision this common stock price pattern as resembling a hockey stick. A long period of relatively sidewise movement along the handle of the stick suddenly takes a sharp curve upward. As in hockey, many sticks break. Some do not.

Part of the common stock price increase may be the elimination of nonmarketability risk at an initial public offering or acquisition by a publicly-traded corporation. Another part of the common stock price rise occurs because business and finance risks embedded in the required rate of return have been reduced. The corporation has separated itself from the many potential venture capital stage failures and established itself as a success. It has trekked through the hazards of the venture capital stage.

Venture capital investors usually cash out after the rapid common stock price rise. Many move onto new venture capital investments. Most venture capital investments fail. Undercapitalization and the lack of entrepreneur stamina are often the causes. Sometimes the idea or product is not well conceived or not well received by its targeted consumer. Delays in achieving envisioned revenues sap the initial enthusiasm of investors and the entrepreneur. Initial funding is spent. More funding is required.[1] Investors may balk. The entrepreneur may simply tire. Yet the venture capital process continues because a few succeed. The successes are sometimes legendary in their extraordinary returns. Examples would be Apple Computer, Microsoft, Intel, Wal-Mart, and Dell Computer. Failures seem to fade into the shadows of the successes.

Most venture capital investments are nonmarketable, although a few have publicly-traded common stock. Infrequently, investors' euphoria for a particular concept, such as the Internet, allows an initial public offering in the venture capital stage. The common stock is publicly sold before a sound operating base for the corporation exists. Payment before product delivery usually attracts numerous public offerings and leads to an abundance of failures in the long term.

As the industry life cycle treks forward through the venture capital stage, the relatively few successes become obvious. Their unique brilliance is usually manifested in very rapid revenue growth and usually high profitability prospects. Their product acceptance grows. The image of an industry and market served is more focused, if not completely defined. Their common stock may be sold to the public, if not already offered. The venture capital stage is left behind. These corporations enter the rapid growth stage.

RAPID GROWTH STAGE

The second stage of the industry life cycle typically witnesses the venture capital firm progressing into a period of rapid growth. The product or service has been developed and marketed to the point of consumer acceptance. The untapped market envisioned by the entrepreneur begins to be tapped. Little competition usually exists for the first to market. The firm faces a wide panorama of demand—a void to be filled. The first successful personal computer manufacturers and the first successful Internet service providers are examples.

The newly-emerged, rapid growth firm usually garners superior profits from untapped and expanding markets. The demand for the product or service probably cannot be meet. The firm can charge high prices without fear of competition. Expected and actual earnings growth is extremely rapid. Investors focus on the expected earnings aspects in their valuations almost to the exclusion of the other factors. Why not? The expected earnings growth is so large that changes in any of the other factors in the Equation (3) valuation framework are usually small by comparison.

The expected earnings in the numerator of the Equation (3) valuation framework are rapidly rising. This swamps the effect of any upward change in interest rates, inflation, equity risk premium, size, business, finance, or marketability risks in the denominator. For example, a relatively large increase in interest rates from 7% to 8%, about a 7.1% change, would have much less effect than a 40% or more upward change in expected earnings on the common stock price valuation. As long as the rapidly increasing expected earnings growth continues, the Equation (3) valuation framework numerator continues to overpower changes in the denominator.

The Equation (3) valuation framework for a rapid growth stage corporation looks like:

$$P = E_1/r + E_2/r + E_3/r \ldots \ldots \ldots E_n/r$$

This represents the present value of the expected earnings each year for the future life of the corporation. Each successive year's earnings will be higher since this is a rapid growth stage company.

The common stock price literally grows into the earnings as time passes, as long as the actual reported earnings meet or exceed expectations. A relatively smaller increase in the required rate of return (r) in the denominator is overpowered. For example, as time passes, a 40% increase in earnings that is now discounted one less year will never be offset by a lesser increased change in the required rate of return. As a year passes, the much larger earnings in year two (E_2) and each successive future year have more upward impact on the common stock price (P) than they did one year earlier. The time discount for which the investor must wait is one year less. The present value of those earnings is greater because the wait is one year shorter. The current common stock price is higher. This process continues as time passes. As the growing expected earnings are realized, the present value is higher.[2]

A rapid growth stage common stock price continues rising as long as the expected earnings are realized. The risk is that expected earnings will not be realized. The downward impact on the stock price is usually immediate and large if realized earnings are less than expected. Not only are the current year's expected earnings reduced, but all future year's expected earnings that have been extrapolated on the large expected growth rate must also be reduced. The impact is cumulative as far as investors can see over the life of the corporation. The present value in each future year is lowered by the reduced earning expectations. The reduction may be very large. The cumulative negative effect on the current common stock price is even larger.

The rapidly growing earnings in the Equation (3) valuation framework do not continue. Competition is attracted by the abnormally high profitability of the first success to emerge from the venture capital stage into the rapid growth stage. Improved product or service variations and/or reduced prices are competitors' entry tactics.

Profit margins fall for all, from the first success to the most recent entering competitor. The first success that gleaned the highest prices and profit margins must lower its prices and profit margins or lose market share. The latest competitive entrants have already reduced prices and profit margins as the cost of entry. All competitors may stay the inevitable decline from abnormally high profits to lower, more normal profits. If there are economies of scale, costs are reduced simultaneously with reduced prices. The rapid expected earnings growth is prolonged. However, market growth, upon which the economies of scale are based, must slow as the market saturates. Production efficiencies must eventually become few and less effective. The rapid growth is over unless underlying technology or other changes reinvigorate production efficiencies and/or the saturated market demand.

The duration of the rapid growth stage for any corporation depends on the ease and speed with which new competitors can enter the market. Throughout the duration of the rapid growth stage, expected earnings are met or exceeded. The common stock price continues to rise. Investors look for industry characteristics associated with prohibiting or delaying competitive entry. These characteristics include the pricing behavior of the first success and the combination of necessity, consumability, and monopoly.

The superior profitability of the first successful entrant into the rapid growth stage partly depends on the high prices it can charge as the only supplier of a product or service to an unsaturated, large, and growing demand. The next entrant usually cuts prices. As long as the first success maintains prices, the competing entrant need not cut its prices any further. On the other hand, if a price war emerges as new competitors enter the market, profit margins shrink, profits fall, and the expected high growth rate in earnings envisioned by investors is jeopardized. Common stock prices fall.

The longest duration in the rapid growth stage is characterized by a combination of necessity, consumability, and monopoly. Necessity fosters purchase. Consumability fosters repurchase. Monopoly fosters repurchase from the one high profit margin producer. If the monopoly becomes too effective and anticompetitive, government regulation usually ensues, and the superior profitability is diminished. Pharmaceutical manufacturers that have strong patents lasting many decades on effective medicines may operate for a while under those characteristics that prolong the rapid growth stage. The image of a critically-ill person turning to the doctor and saying "No thanks, I will wait for the development of competing drugs to lower the price" is not realistic. Necessity mandates the patient buys the drug. Consumability mandates the patient buys the drug again. The producer's protected patent position mandates the patient buys the drug from it.

Investors look for numerous techniques that discourage competitive entry. Brand identification and loyalty are cultivated so that consumers specifically request and are willing to pay a higher price for the brand relative to its generic competitor. Few ask the grocery store clerk for facial tissues while many ask for Kleenex, a brand name. Few with bleeding cuts on their arm run down the hall asking for a plastic adhesive bandage, while many ask for a BandAid, a brand name. Few ask for a cola, while many ask for Coke, a brand name. The successful differentiation of the product in the consumer's mind prolongs the rapid growth stage.

Superior distribution channels and techniques prolong the rapid growth stage. Avon Products overcame the limits of a relatively untrained sales force through door-to-door personalized selling. The long-term personal interaction between the customer and the salesperson, often at relatively low compensation per hour, fostered a unique, profitable distribution channel. However, the inevitable change in society that sent the "at home" customer to work narrowed the Avon distribution channel and profits. Commanding shelf space for consumer products in retail stores, Internet e-commerce sites with customer loyalty, and larger Wal-Mart stores using quantity purchasing power to underprice single-unit local merchants are a few examples.

Physical limitations sometimes discourage new competitive entrants. The first cable television service in the area tends to be the only cable television service in the area. The cost of overlaying a competing cable service may be prohibitive to a second entrant. Yet the inevitable entrepreneurship of the capitalistic system will encourage competition, such as satellite television, to speed the cable industry through the rapid growth stage.

Superior technology may discourage competition and prolong the rapid growth stage. Faster, more powerful computer chips, unique software programs, and superior cement formulations are examples. The money market fund and the cash management account superseded the prosaic passbook savings account.

The continuing combination of necessity, consumability, and monopoly prolongs the rapid growth stage. The failure to maintain one of the components causes diminished earnings growth prospects and abruptly lowers the common stock price. The Polaroid instant camera had the technological monopoly. The courts upheld that position and helped force the Kodak instant camera off the market. Yet Polaroid earnings growth faltered because the product was not particularly consumable and was susceptible to new technology. The instant camera market saturated. The video camera was more appealing.

THE SHAKEOUT

The end of the rapid growth stage is typically marked by the "shakeout," as denoted in Figure 6.1. The flood of new competitors, the accompanying product or service price deterioration, the introduction of superior technology and distribution, and/or any other circumstances that lower entry barriers eliminate the superior profitability and diminish earnings growth prospects. Weaker competitors fall. The stronger firms survive and consolidate. The most efficient, best, least expensive operating characteristics developed in the competitive fight are adopted. The industry is more uniform.

The trek from the first success entering the rapid growth stage to the shakeout has similarities across industries and time. The infant automobile industry in the late nineteenth century had at least three technologically different cars: steam driven, electric driven, and gas driven. The competing cars slugged it out until the gas engine emerged as the most efficient. The Stanley Steamer and other steam and electric cars disappeared.

Competing operating models for the gas-driven car remained. The economics of the industry changed after Henry Ford developed the assembly line. Inefficient manufacturers were driven out of business or into consolidation with those who had the resources and the foresight to adopt the assembly line. The formation of General Motors and its more consumer-oriented cars, besides the famous black color of the Model T, sped the shakeout. The industry lost the Reo, Marmon, Studebaker, Nash, Kaiser, Packard, and many more. The big three automakers emerged.

Other examples of shakeouts occurred in fast-food outlets and home shopping. The first fast-food outlet on the corner generated superior expected earnings growth. Others followed until there was an outlet on at least three of the four corners at any intersection. Each tried to maintain the price by differentiating the sauce, the shape, the cooking style, etc. Eventually prices were cut. The less efficient went bankrupt. The strong remained. The trek from the beginning of the rapid growth stage to the shakeout took only a few years.

The shakeout in television home shopping took only months. Home-shopping operations sprouted. Anybody with access to cheap television time and "slocky" merchandise appeared. There were not enough eyeballs sitting at home to view all the home-shopping programs. The weak failed. The strong quickly consolidated into the few.

The shakeout usually materializes suddenly. Common stock prices fall quickly and sharply. The Equation (3) valuation framework reflects this with a sharp drop in expected earnings in every future year. The negative impact of each year's drop is cumulative. Investors realize the superior growth and profitability will not continue. The rapid growth stage is over. The strong consolidate. The weak disappear. Investors are faced with a few solid firms within a more clearly defined industry.

THE MATURE STAGE

Companies in the mature stage of the industry life cycle are entrenched in the economic mainstream. Their products, brands, distribution channels, and other aspects of their operations are established. Many become blue chips. Some become giants in their industry. Basic operating characteristics standardize among firms within an industry. Financial positions are more liquid and solidly supported within accepted industry standards.

The markets served are no longer unsaturated. Mature firms must depend on reaching the more marginal customers at competitively low prices, replacing and updating sales to prior customers, and most importantly, sustained general economic growth. Profits are more dependent on efficient, low-cost production than on an "any price the market will bear" approach used during the previously unsatiated demand of the rapid growth stage. The superior rates of earnings growth of the rapid growth stage decelerate.

The shift to general economic growth as the driving force behind mature stage company sales and profits means expected earnings are more sensitive to business cycle fluctuations. Mature stage companies can no longer plow unaffected through the recession. Their demand and pricing strength is no longer so well supported by the unsaturated market. The loss of a few marginal customers, unable to afford the firm's product or service because of the recession, adversely affects sales. This marginal loss previously did not matter in the rapid growth stage because companies were not able to supply all demand. Now, as mature stage companies serving a mature market, the loss of the few marginal customers affects their sales and profits.

The demand for mature stage company products or services grows less rapidly. The rate of growth is more affected by the business cycle. Recessions bring slower growth and lower expected earnings. Higher fixed-cost companies, which cannot reduce costs in response to the recession, suffer deeper earnings declines. Higher variable-cost companies suffer more sallow declines in expected earnings. General economic expansions bring faster and higher expected earnings recovery to high fixed-cost than to high variable-cost companies.

Fluctuations in the expected earnings of mature stage companies cause fluctuations in their common stock prices. Expected earnings are no longer in the continuous high-growth rate uptrend of the rapid growth stage. Sales and earnings growth trend down to the general economic growth rate. Recessions or expansions below or above the long-term economic growth trend decelerate or accelerate expected earnings. The degree of change reflects the magnitude of the economic cycle. Sharp decelerations or accelerations in expected earnings are unlikely in most mature stage companies.

Change in expected earnings for mature stage companies affects the numerator in the Equation (3) valuation framework. The present value concept remains the same. The rate of change in expected earnings directly affects the common stock price. Declining earnings exert downward pressure on the common stock price. Rising earnings exert upward pressure on the common stock price. Conversely a rising required rate of return, particularly interest rates, exerts downward pressure on the common stock price. A falling required rate of return exerts upward pressure on the common stock price. The interaction between the rate of change in expected earnings in the numerator and the rate of change in the required rate of return in the denominator of the Equation (3) valuation framework determines the direction and magnitude of the change in the common stock price.

The rate of change in the expected earnings in the numerator relative to the rate of change in the required rate of return in the denominator, particularly interest rates, are distinctly different in the mature stage compared to the rapid growth stage. Mature stage companies' expected earnings grow less rapidly and fluctuate more in-line with the business cycle. Rapid growth stage companies' expected earnings, in contrast, grow more rapidly and fluctuate less in-line with the business cycle. Investors expect smaller rates of change in the earnings of mature stage companies. During periods of relatively large interest rate fluctuations, the rate of change in expected earnings for the mature stage companies is less than the rate of change in the interest-rate-driven required rate of return in the denominator of the Equation (3) valuation framework. Again the impact on the common stock price depends on the direction and relative rates of change in the numerator and the denominator of the Equation (3) valuation framework.

Investors observe significant impacts on mature stage companies' common stock prices from both the numerator and the denominator in the Equation (3) valuation framework. In contrast, rapid growth stage companies' common stock prices are more affected by their overpowering growth in expected earnings. Interest rates have a relatively lower rate of change. The rate of change in the Equation (3) valuation framework numerator is greater than the rate of change in the denominator for the rapid growth stage companies. As the industry passes from the rapid growth stage through its shakeout into the mature stage, the relative degree of impact shifts from a numerator-driven change in expected earnings to a more balanced impact from both numerator and denominator changes in the mature stage.

Risks for mature stage common stock investors arise from the relative changes in expected earnings and interest rates as the economic/stock price cycle progresses. Mature stage common stocks comprise most of the common stock indexes used to describe "the market." Their collective, broad-based movements are the market.

At the beginning of a bull market, interest rates remain cyclically low while expected earnings of mature stage companies start to increase with economic recovery prospects. Investors gravitate first to these more economically entrenched companies because they are envisioned as the first to experience regenerated earnings growth as well as the most likely to remain financially solid if the incipient recovery fails to materialize.

The bull market in mature stage company common stock prices continues as long as their expected earnings increase more rapidly than the more laggard increase in interest rates. This is observed in Stages I and II of the economic/stock price cycle.

A bear market for mature stage common stock prices, as reflected in the broad-based common stock indexes, starts when the rate of increase in the expected earnings is less than the rate of increase in interest rates. This is observed throughout Stage III in the economic/stock price cycle. The bear market continues in Stage IV, the recession phase of the economic/stock price cycle, as long as the rate of decrease in expected earnings is greater than the rate of decrease in interest rates.

Companies progress through the mature stage toward the stable/declining stage. Expected earnings growth tapers off until stabilizing or declining at the end of the mature stage. Demand for the product or service becomes more rigidly defined and static. The few consolidated companies in the industry cannot grow the demand. They all suffer declining earnings expectations in recessions. They compete among themselves for market share. The demand for their product or service shrinks as competing products or services erode the static market. The typewriter gives way to the stand alone word processor that, in turn, gives way to the personal computer. The tin can is replaced by the aluminum can. The tramlines give way to the car. The replaced industries decline to their minimum level of existence and may disappear.

THE STABLE/DECLINING STAGE

Companies in the stable/declining stage of their industry life cycle exhibit steady to declining expected earnings. Investors emphasize expected dividends in their valuation. Dividend yield must provide the bulk of the required rate of return. Little common stock price appreciation is expected since there is little expected earnings growth to cause the common stock price to rise.

The expected earnings in the numerator in the Equation (3) valuation framework are either stable or declining. Most of the earnings are distributed as dividends. Companies in this life cycle stage usually have few attractive capital-investment opportunities. Growth prospects are limited. Dividends are more attractive than retained earnings. A pattern of stable earnings and dividends develops. The numerator of the Equation (3) valuation framework resembles a bond—constant without growth.

Change in the stable/declining stage company's common stock price usually originates from change in the interest rate component of the required rate of return in the denominator of the Equation (3) valuation framework. Like a bond the stable/declining common stock price fluctuates inversely with interest rates. Relatively small rates of change in interest rates exceed the little, if any, rate of change in the relatively stable expected earnings. The stable expected earnings of traditional electric utilities, for example, make their common stock prices sensitive to the rate of change in interest rates. Their common stock prices fall when interest rates rise during inflation and economic expansion. Conversely their common stock prices rise during the low and falling interest rate environment of recessions. These stable expected earnings companies are often referred to as "interest-rate-sensitive stocks."

Investors are not only alert to the common stock price change caused by interest rate fluctuations but are also particularly sensitive to signs that expected dividends may wither. Dividend capacity measures, such as dividend coverage and liquidity reserves, are scrutinized. Many stable dividends have disappeared. The U.S. television manufacturing industry, trolley cars, and the horse-and-buggy trade are examples. Firms sometimes reinvest themselves, delaying or even preventing the trek through the mature stage into decline. IBM reinvested itself as a computer service company, switching emphasis from mainframe computers that had been losing ground to servers, routers, PCs and similar technological advances.

SUMMARY

Industries develop different characteristics that affect the relative influence of the numerator or the denominator of the Equation (3) valuation framework on the common stock price. Survival is paramount through the venture capital stage. Management stamina and cash must be sufficient to support survival until the firm passes into the rapid growth stage.

Expected earnings growth dominates investors' valuation analysis in the rapid growth stage. Expected earnings growth is changing so rapidly upward that it overpowers changes in the other Equation (3) valuation framework factors. The major risk in this stage is that expected earnings do not materialize. Eventually so much competition is attracted that the weak fall in an industry shakeout. The survivors consolidate into a more homogeneous industry and enter the mature stage.

The rate of change in expected earnings in the numerator and in the required rate of return in the denominator of the Equation (3) valuation framework become a more balanced focus of investors in the mature stage. Expected earnings grow less rapidly and fluctuate more in association with the business cycle. The relative changes in expected earnings and in the required rate of return affect the common stock price. Mature stage companies are more established in the economy and are the largest segment of investment grade common stocks.

Industries and companies advance through the mature stage until pushed into the stable/declining stage by newer, more dynamic companies. Revenues and expected earnings stagnate and decline. Investors emphasize dividends and current yield over growth. Stable/declining stage common stock prices change more in response to the rates of change in interest rates than to their smaller rate of change in expected earnings. Common stocks with stable expected earnings, such as traditional electrical utilities, behave more like bonds than stocks because the rate of change in their expected earnings is less than the rate of change in interest rates.

NOTES

1. Investors judge the firm's funding needs by the "cash burn rate"—the speed at which cash is spent. High cash burn rates are often associated with additional funding needs or insolvency or undercapitalized firms. Infrequently, high common stock valuations may provide a temporary "currency" with which to raise additional funds.

2. This is the Petersburg Paradox. The present value (current common stock price) is infinite if the rate of growth in expected earnings always exceeds the discount rate (the required rate of return). Investors never observe this paradox because all firms eventually have their expected earnings growth rate decelerate and drop below the required rate of return.

7

The Price/Earnings Multiple

How does the price/earnings multiple behave over the industry life cycle?

The price/earnings multiple is an encapsulation of the present value concept embodied in the Equation (3) valuation framework. Investors cannot forecast earnings accurately, if at all, very far into the future. Yet the common stock price is the present value of all future earnings over the assumed perpetual life of the company. Through necessity or convenience, investors have become relatively myopic. They have adopted the price/earnings multiple as a contraction to approximate the concept of the Equation (3) valuation framework.

The price/earnings multiple, or P/E as it is usually called, is the reciprocal of the required rate of return (r) in the denominator of the Equation (3) valuation framework when the expected earnings in the numerator are constant:

P/E = 1/r

This is demonstrated in Appendix 7A.

The P/E responds inversely to changes in the required rate of return. Since the largest and most frequent percentage change in the required rate of return tends to be interest rates, the P/E fluctuates as interest rates fluctuate. Rising interest rates cause falling P/Es and vice versa. This is particularly true for a well-diversified common stock portfolio that has mitigated company-specific risks.

The common stock price is the P/E times the most applicable, concurrent, one-year earnings (E_1), instead of all future years, expected earnings as in the Equation (3) valuation framework:

$$P = P/E * E_1 \tag{4}$$

Equation (4) is often called the P/E valuation model.

Some investors use trailing twelve-month earnings. Other investors use next year's expected earnings consensus. Still others use their own forecasts. The effect is the same regardless of which single-year earnings are used. The common stock price valuation concept remains grounded in the present value of expected earnings. The P/E reflects the required rate of return in the Equation (3) valuation framework.

Common stock prices fluctuate as the P/E multiple contracts or expands in response to changes in the components of the required rate of return. As the required rate of return increases, the P/E decreases and vice versa. The common stock price follows. For example, as interest rates rise, the P/E falls as does the common stock price, provided expected earnings do not change. This relationship holds in combination 4 of Table 1.1 and in the Equation (3) valuation framework. As interest rates fall, the P/E rises as does the common stock price, provided expected earnings do not change. This relationship holds in combination 3 of Table 1.1 and in the Equation (3) valuation framework. The P/E multiple is said to have expanded or contracted in response to falling or rising interest rates.

The common stock price also responds to changes in earnings in the P/E valuation model, as seen in equation (4). Rising single-year expected earnings cause common stock prices to rise, provided the P/E has not fallen more in response to rising interest rates or other required rate of return factors. This relationship holds in combinations 1 and 8a of Table 1.1 and in the Equation (3) valuation framework. Falling single-year expected earnings cause the common stock price to fall, provided the P/E has not risen more in response to falling interest rates. This relationship holds in combinations 7 and 9a of Table 1.1 and in the Equation (3) valuation framework.

P/E IMPLICATIONS AND POTENTIAL DISTORTIONS

Potential distortions are created because investors' myopia, caused by their inability to forecast accurately expected earnings in perpetuity, is embedded in the P/E valuation model. The Equation (3) valuation framework time horizon truncates to a single-year expected earnings while the common stock price still reflects the present value of all future expected earnings.

The growth rate in expected earnings for growth stocks is often assumed constant at any time in the P/E valuation model. This limits the P/E model. Cyclical fluctuations in expected earnings for business-cycle-sensitive companies are not accurately captured in the single-year P/E valuation model. Earnings deficits, particularly of venture capital stage companies, are not conceptually captured in the P/E valuation model. Companies worth more for their assets than for their earnings capacity cannot be conceptually or accurately valued in the P/E model.

Growth Stocks

The P/E multiple for growth stocks is distorted by the truncation of the Equation (3) valuation framework. The common stock price (P) in the numerator of the P/E multiple reflects all future earnings discounted to the present. In contrast, the earnings (E) in the P/E multiple reflect only relatively current single-year earnings in the denominator. The comparison is "apples to oranges." The price in the numerator reflects the entire future. The earnings in the denominator reflect only a relatively current single year.

The current common stock price of a growth company reflects the cumulative impact of much higher earnings expected years from now. The current earnings are low. The P/E is high. For example, a rapid growth stage company's expected earnings might resemble:

Year	Earnings per Share ($)
1	.01
2	.10
3	1.00
4	4.00
5	8.00
6	16.00
7	32.00

The common stock price might be about $180 based on a 20% required rate of return. The P/E would be 18,000 based on the year 1 earnings, 1,800 based on year 2 projected earnings, and 180 based on year 3 projected earnings. All these P/Es would be considered high by historical average standards. They are not incorrect. They are simply distorted by the P/E truncation of the Equation (3) valuation framework. The common stock price reflects the value from the envisioned earnings over the life of the company. The P/E valuation model reflects the common stock price relative only to the current earnings. An apples-to-oranges distortion occurs.

The risk in a high P/E multiple growth stock is not necessarily the high valuation but the failure of earnings to meet expectations. Once the growth rate is not maintained, expected earnings in every future year are adjusted down. The cumulative effect is a sharp drop in the common stock price. Of course there is some P/E at which the valuation is too high even if the expected earnings are realized.

Cyclical Stocks

The P/E truncation of the Equation (3) valuation framework also distorts its interpretation when applied to cyclical stocks. Cyclical expected earnings patterns fluctuate even if generally trending upward. Cyclical common stocks are business-cycle-sensitive and in the mature or stable/declining stage of their industry life cycle. Their P/E may be high during a year of recession-depressed, temporarily low earnings. Investors look beyond the valley in earnings to the earnings recovery. Conversely a cycle stock P/E may be low during expansion-induced, temporarily high earnings. Investors look over the mountain to the next valley in earnings. For example, projected cyclical earnings could be as follows:

Year	Earnings per Share ($)
1	.01
2	1.00
3	5.00
4	1.00
5	.01
6	4.00
7	8.00

In this case, the common stock price might be about $48. The P/E would be over 4,800 based on year 1 earnings, 48 based on year 2 projected earnings, and 9.6 based on year 3 projected earnings. The first seems too high. The last seems low by historical standards. They are not incorrect. They are simply distorted.

The cause of distortion in the P/E multiple is the same as for a growth stock. The common stock price reflects all future earnings. The P/E valuation model uses only the current single-year earnings in its denominator. Investors are again faced with the apples-to-oranges comparison.

Deficits

The P/E multiple truncation becomes meaningless when there are no earnings. Earnings in the denominator of the P/E valuation model are negative. The P/E multiple is also negative. Rigid application of the P/E model implies a negative common stock price. This implies selling stockholders must pay buying stockholders to take the shares off their hands. This is illogical. A negative P/E multiple also becomes less negative as earnings deficits enlarge. This is also illogical.

The positive common stock price for a company with a current earnings deficit reflects positive future earnings discounted to the present as in the Equation (3) valuation framework. This is not captured in the P/E valuation model. The P/E is not meaningful for a common stock with a current earnings deficit.

Companies with earnings deficits have no meaningful P/E. Sometimes another valuation shorthand is used, such as the price/revenues multiple in the early stages of the Internet stocks. This multiple may have less specific meaning because minority position common stock prices are based on earnings and not revenues. There is little comfort in knowing that because one Internet stock sells for two hundred times revenues, others in the industry must also sell at that multiple of revenues.

Assets

The value of a few companies lies more in the worth of their assets than in the expected earnings generated from those assets. These firms are worth more "dead than alive." Controlling stockholders can profit by liquidating or selling the assets. Minority position stockholders cannot force such a liquidation or sale upon entrenched and intransigent boards of directors. Shareholders may never realize the asset value underlying the shares. The common stock price is based on the expected poor earnings generated from the underperforming assets and is less than the value of the assets themselves.

The same potential distortions exist for any valuation framework that truncates and approximates the Equation (3) valuation framework. All valuation frameworks, however, must truncate. Investors simply cannot accurately forecast expected earnings until infinity. No human can. Successful entrepreneurs may correctly envision trends, but they can no more precisely forecast expected earnings than anyone else. Many entrepreneurs correctly forecast the large future trends and succeed. Others fail. Wall Street analysts are rated for the accuracy of their one-year future earnings forecasts. The more accurate ones are lauded and rewarded well. However, consistent accuracy is not one of their common characteristics.

Investors must recognize the potential P/E distortion and the associated risks and valuation implications. Investors must also respond appropriately. For example, many investors diversify.

GENERAL STOCK MARKET BUBBLES AND SINKHOLES

When looking at the diversified portfolio of common stocks known as the stock market, investors can draw some implications about the general market consensus for expected earnings growth, duration for earnings growth, and valuation. These implications are revealed when investors judge the expected return/risk relationship in the P/E.

Investors understand that the interest rate risk, including inflation, and the equity risk premium are always present, even in a well-diversified portfolio. The risk of expected earnings not materializing cannot be diversified away. The equity risk premium remains. Otherwise the perfectly diversified portfolio of common stocks has the same certainty as the U.S. Treasury bond. Most of this chapter's insights apply to general common stock market valuation. Some more limited insights also apply to specific common stock valuation.

Implied Growth Rate

The P/E valuation model, in contrast to the explicit identification of the Equation (3) valuation framework, implies an assumed expected earnings growth rate that is not explicitly obvious in the P/E calculation. A general market P/E of 20, for example, implies a 5% required of return without any expected earnings growth. The implied rate of return, as judged by the reciprocal of the P/E, is 5%. A P/E of 40 implies a required rate of return of only 2.5%, if there were no expected earnings growth. Under these assumed required rates of return, rapidly growing companies' returns would not be worth the risk unless investors foresaw higher expected earnings. Yet the P/E valuation framework incorporates no explicit growth factor. The valuation implicitly assumes an expected growth that varies among investors and may not materialize. The common stock price would be much lower and the implied required rate of return much higher if no expected earnings growth were anticipated.

The P/E conceals an implied expected earnings growth rate for an assumed time horizon. For example, the combination of a P/E of 30 based on trailing twelve-month earnings and a P/E of 20 based on one-year forward expected earnings implies a 50% one-year growth rate. Investors can compare the implied growth rate to the consensus expected earnings growth rate. An implied growth rate higher than the expected consensus growth rate might imply an overextended common stock market and vice versa.

Estimating the implied growth rate in expected earnings from the general common stock market P/E provides a sanity check. The difference between the current P/E based on current earnings and next year's P/E based on projected earnings implies a growth rate. An extremely high implied earnings growth might not be realistically attainable. The stock market index may be vulnerable. For example, a current general market P/E of 40 compared to a projected P/E of 20 implies a 100% growth rate in earnings in one year. The implied compound growth rate is over 41% in two years and decreases over a longer time horizon. An increase in interest rates and/or equity risk premium necessitates a still higher growth rate to offset their declining impact on the P/E multiples.

Implied Required Rate of Return

The P/E implies a general market required rate of return when a time horizon and an expected earnings growth rate are assumed. For example, assuming a one-year time horizon and a 10% expected earnings growth rate, a common stock market index with a P/E of 20 has an implied 15% required rate of return. The required return must be large enough to discount the 10% expected earnings growth in the numerator and the implied 5% required rate of return in the denominator of the Equation (3) valuation framework. The implied 5% in the denominator is the reciprocal of the observed P/E 20, with no earnings growth.

The 15% required rate of return is the minimum required return on a perfectly diversified common stock portfolio that has eliminated all company-specific risks. Such a portfolio may not be attainable. That does not detract from the insights of the analysis. Further, as long as the equity risk premium above the default-free interest rate remains the same, only changes in the expected earnings growth rate and in the interest rate affect the implied change in the estimated growth rate.

Coincidentally the long-run return to the common stock market has been about 12%. The sum of a 5% long-term U.S. Treasury bond yield and an average 7% long-horizon general equity risk premium is also 12%. The 5% yield for the long-term U.S. Treasury bond and a 7% long-horizon equity risk premium are historically realistic.

The nongrowth P/E based on the reciprocal of this implied 12% required rate of return is 8.3. The difference between the implied long-term, nongrowth P/E of 8.3 and a higher observed P/E reflects expected earnings growth. An expected 6% earnings growth rate in earnings reduces the required rate of return from 12% to 6% and implies a P/E of 16.7. Higher expected earnings growth implies still higher P/Es.

Investors sometimes calculate the nongrowth P/E as the reciprocal of interest rates, excluding the equity risk premium. For example, a 5% long-term U.S. Treasury bond interest rate implies a P/E of 20, representing the reciprocal of that interest rate.

Implied Time Horizon Duration

Investors can gauge the duration of expected earnings growth when they assume a growth rate and an interest rate. This analysis may be the easiest to estimate and the most insightful. The required information is a consensus expected earnings growth rate and the current default-risk-free U.S. Treasury bond yield. The former can be readily obtained from available earnings surveys. The latter can be observed in the bond market.

Investors must compute the estimated default-risk-free, nongrowth value for the stock market index and compare that to the prevailing stock market index. The estimated default-risk-free, nongrowth value is approximated by multiplying the stock market current earnings times the nongrowth P/E, judged as the reciprocal of the U.S. Treasury bond yield. The current common stock market index is typically higher because it incorporates expected earnings growth. The difference between the estimated default-risk-free, nongrowth common stock market valuation and the higher prevailing common stock market index reflects the embedded expected earnings.

Investors then take the consensus earnings growth rate and determine the duration needed for that growth rate to make up the difference between the current and implied embedded expected earnings. Very high duration implies investors are very optimistic and confident about future growth. They are willing to pay higher common stock prices justified on expected earnings growth far into the future (See Appendix 7B).

High duration exposes the stock market to a greater possibility of expected earnings disappointment and often accompanies peaks in stock market bubbles that soon burst. For example, an estimated default-risk-free, nongrowth index value of 10,000 compared to an actual index value of 13,000 implies a 30% increase in expected earnings growth. At a consensus 10% growth rate, duration would be three years or twelve quarters. Studies (See Chapter 8) show this is often at the edge of a bursting bubble. The same studies also show that very low implied duration usually foreshadows a stock market recovery.

OTHER VALUATION SHORTHANDS

Investors sometimes truncate the Equation (3) valuation framework using other indications of expected $Benefits to be received. Under the assumption that sales lead to earnings that, in turn, lead to dividends, investors may use a price/sales valuation multiple. The common stock price may be incorrectly valued if this sequence does not occur.

Sales are sometimes the only indication of expected $Benefits. For example, companies in the early growth stages of the Internet industry had no earnings. Their price/earnings multiples were meaningless, as already noted. Investors turned to the price/sales multiple as a valuation guide. Internet common stocks were selling upwards of two hundred times sales in anticipation of rapidly growing and high earnings yet to come. Failure to meet expected sales growth and levels sent common stock prices plummeting, as is similar to high P/E common stocks that fail to meet earnings expectations. The same potential distortions exist in any shorthand of the Equation (3) valuation framework.

Investors sometimes use other truncated valuation multiples with different indications of expected $Benefits. The price/cash flow multiple uses cash flow, often measured as the earnings before interest, taxes, depreciation and amortization (EBITDA). Investors sometimes use a price multiple of free cash flow, judged as cash flow less capital expenditures and dividends. A price multiple of an unweighted or weighted average of past years is used in the valuation of cyclical stocks to smooth earnings fluctuation to a more fundamental earnings capacity less affected by the business cycle. The price/book multiple is also used, particularly for common stocks where asset-based valuations are more appropriately emphasized.

The P/E multiple is sometimes divided by the company's growth rate (G) to derive the PE/G multiple. This attempts to standardize the rapid growth stage valuation multiple among the different earnings growth rates. The more rapidly growing companies have a higher P/E multiple distortion because their common stock prices reflect the higher expected earnings relative to their current lower earnings. This P/E distortion is mitigated by the PE/G multiple. The PE/G indicates how long it would take the expected earnings growth to compensate for the implicit growth embedded in the P/E. The PE/G suffers the same potential distortions as any other shorthand of the Equation (3) valuation framework. Failure to meet expected earnings growth adversely affects the common stock price.

COMPARATIVE VS. DYNAMIC P/E ANALYSIS

Investors may use the P/E valuation framework as a static comparative analysis and may miss its inherent dynamics. Common stock P/E multiples are ranked in ascending or descending order. Common stocks within an industry usually cluster around a similar P/E multiple, particularly in the mature stage of their industry life cycle when operations are relatively homogeneous. Investors start their valuations of common stocks within an industry at the industry average P/E multiple and then adjust that P/E for favorable or unfavorable individual company characteristics or risks.

This P/E adjustment process provides a comparative, relative valuation ranking. For example, the aluminum industry may have only a handful of producers. New entrants are unlikely because of the high entry cost and saturated market. Investors compare the operating and financial profiles of all the companies. One company, however, may have less business risk because of entrenched market share, markets served, greater production efficiency, lower financial leverage, better management record, etc. The "better profile" company receives a higher than industry average P/E valuation. The "worse than average profile" company receives a lower than industry average P/E valuation.

The comparative P/E valuation analysis misses an important dynamic that is captured in the Equation (3) valuation framework. The entire P/E ranking may shift for all companies within an industry. The same relative, comparative rankings remain, but the average P/E for the entire industry rises or falls in response to changes in general valuation factors, such as interest rates and inflation. A company's common stock price based on its relative ranking to the current industry average P/E may look undervalued or overvalued. However, the cheap stock of today based on a P/E relatively lower than the prevailing industry average P/E or common stock market P/E may be even cheaper tomorrow. The stock price and the P/E may be lower but in the same relative position to a lower industry average P/E multiple or general common stock market P/E. The current relative, comparative P/E rankings of common stocks within the industry have not changed. The entire P/E range has shifted.

SUMMARY

The Equation (3) valuation framework is truncated to the P/E, or other similar valuation multiple, because investors are unable to foresee expected earnings over the life of a company. Investors must understand the potential distortion that this causes. Very high, almost meaningless, P/Es often result for growth stocks. The number in the P/E numerator reflects the expected earnings in every year of the assumed perpetual life of the company. The earnings in the P/E denominator reflect only a single current year, typified by much lower earnings yet to grow. Similar distortions occur in cyclical common stocks, deficit earnings, and asset-oriented P/E valuations.

The P/E shorthand contains some insights into general market valuations. The general market index P/E without growth is the reciprocal of a combined, appropriate interest rate and equity risk premium. Any market index level above that must be justified by expected earnings growth. Investors judge the time (duration) it would take at current earnings growth rates to close the gap between the estimated nongrowth common stock price index and the prevailing common stock price index. Common stock market bubbles are associated with implied long-growth duration. Market index sinkholes are associated with implied short-growth duration.

Appendix 7A

The Nongrowth Price/Earnings Multiple Derived

The nongrowth P/E is the reciprocal of the required rate of return, identified as the denominator of the Equation (3) valuation framework. The common stock price is the present value of the dividends derived from the expected earnings over the assumed infinite life of the company as reflected in Equation (3):

$$P = \sum_{t=1,\infty} E_t(1 - \Lambda) / (1 + r)^t \tag{3}$$

P   = common stock price

$\sum_{t=1,\infty}$ = sum of all expected earnings in each year t

E_t = expected earnings in each year t

Λ = a constant earnings retention rate

r   = the required rate of return

Assuming constant expected earnings, the numerator of the equation above does not change. The denominator changes as the factors in r, the required rate of return, change. Those factors are interest rates, including inflation, and an equity risk premium for a common stock market index.

The factors expand to include company-specific risks, such as size, business, financial, and marketability risks for individual common stocks. These general and company-specific risk components of the required rate of return have already been identified in the denominator of the Equation (3) valuation framework. The common stock price may also be expressed without the summation sign of Equation (3) to form equation (3a):

$$P = E_1 / (1 + r)^1 + E_2 / (1 + r)^2 + E_3 / (1 + r)^3 + \ldots \ldots \ldots$$
$$\ldots E_n / (1 + r)^n \qquad (3a)$$

where E is constant, nongrowth expected earnings in each year of the company's infinite life.

Multiplying both sides of equation (3a) by $(1 + r)$ results in equation (3b):

$$(1 + r) P = E + E / (1 + r)^1 + E / (1 + r)^2 +$$
$$\ldots \ldots \ldots \ldots \ldots \ldots \ldots \ldots \ldots \ldots \ldots E / (1 + r)^{n-1} \qquad (3b)$$

Subtracting equation (3a) from equation (3b) results in equation (3c):

$$(1 + r)P - P = E - E / (1 + r)^n \qquad (3c)$$

Combining terms in equation (3c) results in equation (3d):

$$rP = E - E / (1 + r)^n \qquad (3d)$$

As n, the number of years, goes to infinity, the second term on the right side of equation (3d) becomes infinitesimally small, disappears, and results in equation (3e):

$$rP = E \qquad (3e)$$

The reciprocal of r in equation (3e) is therefore equation (3f):

$$P/E = 1 / r \qquad (3f)$$

The P/E is the reciprocal of the required rate of return for nongrowth, constant earnings common stocks. It is also the cost of equity capital when expected earnings are held constant.

Appendix 7B

The Default-Risk-Free, Nongrowth Time Horizon Duration

The difference between the observed current common stock price (P) and its theoretical default-risk-free nongrowth value (S_{ng}) is:

$$P - S_{ng} \tag{7B}$$

where S_{ng} is:

$$S_{ng} = \Sigma_{t=1, \infty} E_t / (1 + r)^t$$

Where E is the expected earnings and r is the default-risk-free, nongrowth return as judged by the long-term U.S. Treasury bond yield. The current common stock price (P) is higher than the nongrowth common stock (S_{ng}) because P embodies expected earnings growth.

The nongrowth common stock value (S_{ng}) must increase in price to equal P to compensate investors for the implied risk premium of owning stocks as opposed to owning U.S. Treasury bonds. Expected earnings growth is the only method by which that compensation can occur.

Investors have an observed current common stock price and calculated difference between S_{ng} and P in equation (7B). Investors also have estimates of expected earnings growth, such as consensus surveys or rates of change in historically recent earnings reports. A time horizon duration is obtained when the difference calculated in equation (7B) is divided by the current consensus growth rate forecast. For example, a 21% difference requires a two-year (eight-quarter) time horizon duration at a 10% compound growth rate in expected earnings.

8

Empirical Studies

The Generation of Stock Market Cycles

Steven E. Bolten;* *University of South Florida*, and Robert A. Weigand, *University of Colorado at Colorado Springs*

ABSTRACT

This paper demonstrates that the relation between stock market and business cycle dynamics can be conceptualized using a dividend discount model. The interaction of changes in earnings and interest rates throughout the economic cycle are shown to cause changes in the level of stock prices. This implies that monitoring and forecasting these factors can help explain and possibly predict stock price behavior over time.

Keywords: business cycle, forecasting, stock prices
JEL Classifications: G14/G10/E32

1. INTRODUCTION

A large body of research has focused on the predictability of stock prices. These researchers invariably find that changes in stock prices are positively related to corporate earnings and negatively related to changes in interest rates, and that the stock market leads the economic cycle. Several studies have attempted to model stock prices and their relationship with earnings and interest rates (Bolten, 1985, 1991; Bolten and Besley, 1986). Other authors (Campbell and Schiller, 1988; Chen, 1991; and Fama, 1981) have shown that the current level of stock prices is related to the discounted value of future earnings and dividends. This paper contributes to our understanding of the valuation process by showing that a basic dividend discount model can capture the interaction between stock prices, corporate earnings and interest rates over time.

The organization of the paper is as follows. The next section provides a brief description of the stock market and economic business

*Corresponding author. The authors would like to thank George Phillippatos and an anonymous reviewer for their helpful comments and suggestions.

cycle. The major factors in the cycle and the interaction among these factors is discussed. Subsequent sections present a dividend discount model and show that this model is consistent with the observed time series behavior of business cycle factors. The final section presents our conclusions.

2. THE STOCK MARKET AND THE ECONOMIC BUSINESS CYCLE

Suppose that the economy starts at a trough and is just about to recover—call this the first stage in the economic cycle (see Figure 1). Expectations are for positive economic growth and higher future earnings, which has a positive impact on stock prices. Interest rates are typically low at this period in the business cycle, which will positively affect stock prices due to a decrease in firms' cost of capital. Low interest rates also induce investors to transfer wealth from low-yielding bonds into stocks, which pushes up stock prices. The combined effect of these factors causes stock prices to rise relatively quickly at this stage, even though the economy may show only marginal signs of improvement.

In the second stage the economy continues to grow and the demand for capital increases. This leads to inflationary pressure and interest rates begin to rise gradually. Expectations of future earnings increase due to the strengthening economy, however. At this stage of the cycle the positive impact of higher earnings expectations dominates the negative impact of higher interest rates. The overall effect on the stock market is positive and prices rise, although not as fast as in the first stage of the economic recovery.

The third stage is characterized by continued economic expansion. The supply of loanable funds cannot keep pace with the increased demand for capital, which causes the rise in interest rates to accelerate. As inflationary concerns worsen the Federal Reserve is likely to tighten monetary policy, which puts more upward pressure on interest rates. Furthermore, the rate of earnings growth begins to slow down due to diminishing marginal productivity. These factors cause a decrease in the rate of economic expansion. Stock prices increase slowly and eventually peak, even though the economy has not yet reached its peak.

Although the economy slows, interest rates may not immediately decrease. Inflationary pressures and the increased costs of financing

Figure 1
Economic Factors and the Stock Market Cycle

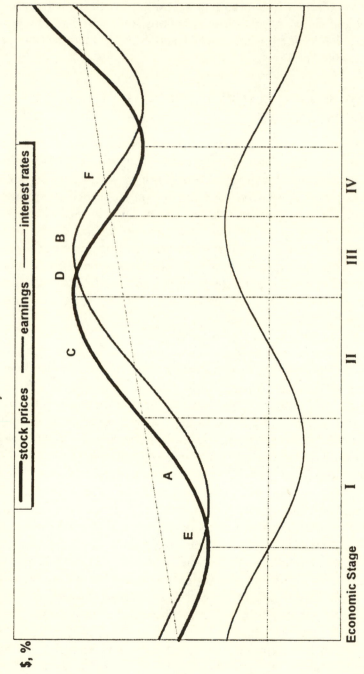

unanticipated inventory accumulations and lagged accounts receivable collection will cause interest rates to continue rising. The combined effect of investors transferring wealth from stocks to bonds and the slow growth in corporate earnings has a negative effect on stock prices.

In the fourth stage worsening economic expectations dim future earnings prospects, which has a negative effect on stock prices. The decreased demand for credit causes interest rates to begin falling. Stock prices will continue to decline until interest rates fall substantially, however. The downtrend in interest rates and improvement in earnings expectations eventually cause a rebound in stock prices.

While brief and necessarily simplified, the above summary of the economic cycle makes several points that are important for the analysis that follows. The interactions between changes in expected future earnings and interest rates determines the direction of stock price changes. When earnings prospects are weak but interest rates are rising, stock prices decline. When earnings expectations are positive (poor) and interest rates are rising (falling) stock prices can either rise or fall, depending on which factor has the relatively larger impact.

3. THE MODEL

The basic dividend discount model is given by:

$$P_0 = \sum_{t=1}^{\infty} \frac{E_t(1 - \lambda)}{(1 + r)^t} \tag{1}$$

which expresses stock prices as the function of an expected earnings stream paid out as dividends discounted to the present at a required rate of return. Equation 1 can be re-written as:

$$P_t = \frac{E_{t+1}(1 - \lambda) + C(1 - \lambda)}{(1 + r_i^*)} \tag{2}$$

where:

E = expectations of next period's corporate earnings. The current set of earnings expectations are formed regarding changes in earnings over the next stage of the economic cycle. In the model, changes in current period economic expectations cause changes in stock prices. This is realistic since it is difficult to forecast earnings for more than a relatively immediate period.

λ = the target retention rate, assumed stable.

C = a constant, representing expectations of total corporate earnings beyond the current business cycle discounted to the end of the current cycle.

r^* = the time-varying interest rate that discounts the expected earnings set $(E_{t+1}(1 - \lambda) + C(1 - \lambda))$ to the current equilibrium level of stock prices.

Since markets are in equilibrium at a given moment in time, the expected interest rate is equal to the current rate (required rate of return). This is also equal to the cost of equity capital. Equation 2 shows that the level of stock prices are positively related to expectations of future earnings and negatively related to interest rates. The next section analyzes deviations from equilibrium that cause stock price fluctuations by modeling the relation between stock prices, earnings and interest rates.

4. ANALYSIS

Taking the derivative of Equation 2 with respect to time yields:

$$\frac{1}{P}\frac{dP}{dt} = \frac{1}{E + C}\frac{dE}{dt} - \frac{1}{(1 + r^*)}\frac{dr}{dt} \qquad (3)$$

Equation 3 reveals that the direction of stock price change is determined by the *relative changes* of expected earnings (a function of the economy) and interest rates (required rate of return in a fungible market context). Table 1 summarizes the following discussion of the comparative static analysis of Equation 3. The last column in Table 1 provides the location of each effect in the business cycle as shown in Figure 1.

When economic activity is increasing ($dE/dt > 0$) and interest rates are falling ($dr/dt < 0$), stock prices will rise ($dP/dt > 0$). The two factors act in the same direction and push the level of stock prices up quickly. This typically occurs close to the economic trough when the stock market is already past its cycle bottom and rising rapidly. This is shown as Period A in Figure 1. The model captures the fact that the stock market bottom leads the economic trough.

When the economy and earnings are expected to decline ($dE/dt < 0$) but interest rates are increasing ($dr/dt > 0$), the level of stock prices

Table 1
The Effect of Changes in Earnings Expectations and Interest Rates on Stock Prices

This table summarizes the implied effects of changes in earnings and interest rates on changes in the level of stock prices as given by Equation 3. The last column in the table gives the location of each effect as shown in Figure 1.

Sign of $\frac{dE}{dt}$ and $\frac{dr}{dt}$		and	implies $\frac{dP}{dt}$	appears in Figure 1 as
+	−		+	A
−	+		−	B
+	+	$(dE/dt) > (dr/dt)(1 + r)(E + C)$	+	C
+	+	$(dr/dt) > (dE/dt)/[(E + C)(1 + r)]$	−	D
−	−	$(dr/dt) > (dE/dt)/[(E + C)(1 + r)]$	+	E
−	−	$(dE/dt) > (dr/dt)(1 + r)(E + C)$	−	F

falls ($dP/dt < 0$). Earnings and interest rates work in the same direction to drive stock prices down. This typically occurs when economic activity is close to its peak. This is shown as Period B in Figure 1. Again, the model captures the fact that stock prices reach their peak before the economy and growth in earnings.

When the economy and earnings are expected to grow ($dE/dt > 0$) and interest rates are rising ($dr/dt > 0$) the general level of stock prices can either rise or fall. If dE/dt is greater than $(dr/dt)(1 + r)$ $(E + C)$, positive earnings expectations have a greater effect on the market than the negative impact of rising interest rates. In this case stock prices rise, although not as fast as when rates are falling. This is represented by Period C in Figure 1. If dr/dt is greater than $(dE/dt)/[(E + C)(1 + r)]$, increasing interest rates have a stronger negative impact on stock prices than positive earnings expectations and stock prices fall. This typically occurs before the peak in economic activity, and is shown as Period D in Figure 1.

When both dr/dt and $dE/dt < 0$, earnings expectations have a negative impact on the stock market but interest rates have a positive impact. Once again, the general level of stock prices can either rise or fall. If $(dr/dt) > (dE/dt)/[(E + C)(1 + r)]$ the impact of falling interest rates is stronger and stock prices rise. If $(dE/dt) > (dr/dt)(1 + r)(E + C)$ the decrease in earnings expectations has a stronger impact and stock prices fall. These are shown as Periods E and F in Figure 1, respectively.[1]

The final scenario (not shown in Table 1 or Figure 1) occurs when $(dE/dt)/(E + C) = (dr/dt)(1 + r)$. In this case the stock market reaches either a peak or trough, depending on the previous direction of price change. That is, the above condition results in a market peak if prices have been rising. If prices have been falling, however, the above condition results in a market bottom.

Table 1 and Figure 1 and the above analysis show that a basic dividend discount model describes the positive relation between stock prices and earnings and the negative relation between stock prices and interest rates. The model shows how economic factors interact to cause changes in stock prices, and captures the manner in which stock market cycles lead economic cycles.

5. CONCLUSIONS

A basic dividend discount model is used to show that characterizing asset prices as the present value of future cash flows is consistent with the observed behavior of economic factors and stock prices. The analysis demonstrates that the interaction of changes in expected earnings and interest rates determine changes in stock prices. The impact of these economic factors on prices depends on both the base level of expected earnings and interest rates and the relative magnitude of changes in these factors. The results imply that monitoring and forecasting economic factors can help explain and possibly predict stock price behavior over time.

REFERENCES

Arnott, R. D., 1990. *Asset Allocation: A Handbook of Portfolio Policies, Strategies and Tactics* (Probus Publishing).

Bolten, S. E., 1985. Cycle exegesis. *Financial Planning* 20, 208–210.

Bolten, S. E., 1991. A note on a dynamic framework for equity price fluctuations. *Working Paper*, University of South Florida.

---

[1]An anonymous reviewer points out that Equation 3 might also be interpreted as a statement about the elasticity of stock prices. Securities prices are known to have greater elasticity when earnings and interest rates are low. Extending the analysis in this fashion is an interesting area for future research.

Bolten, S. E., and S. Besley, 1986. Long-term asset allocation under dynamic interaction of earnings and interest rates. *The Financial Review* 26, 269–274.

Campbell, J. Y., and R. J. Schiller, 1988. The dividend price ratio and expectations of future dividends and discount factors. *Review of Financial Studies* 1, 195–228.

Campbell, J. Y., and R. J. Schiller, 1988. Stock prices, earnings, and expected dividends. *Journal of Finance* 43, 661–676.

Chen, N., 1991. Financial investment opportunities and the macroeconomy. *Journal of Finance* 46, 529–554.

Fama, E. F., 1981. Stock returns, real activity, inflation and money. *American Economic Review* 82, 545–565.

Farrell, J. L., 1986. Fundamental forecast approach to superior asset allocation. *Financial Analysts Journal* 42, 32–37.

Harlow, W. V., 1991. Asset allocation in a downside-risk framework. *Financial Analysts Journal* 48, 28–40.

Marmer, H. S., 1991. Optional international asset allocation under different economic environments: a Canadian perspective. *Financial Analysts Journal* 48, 85–92.

Perold, A., and W. Sharpe, 1988. Dynamic strategies for asset allocation. *Financial Analysts Journal* 44, 16.

Weigel, E. J., 1991. The performance of tactical asset allocation. *Financial Analysts Journal* 48, 63–70.

A Note on Cyclical and Dynamic Aspects of Stock Market Price Cycles*

Steven E. Bolten and Susan W. Long*

INTRODUCTION

Almost all economic and financial data are cyclically oriented and not attuned to any chronological or calendar rigid time frame. Yet, most financial market data and studies use empirical data based on time specific data. By necessity, therefore, these models of security price movements are general equilibrium or, at best, comparative static equilibrium positions without explanations of the movement through the cycle of stock prices [8, 9, 10, 11]. This note examines the cyclical dynamics of stock market prices in a general market analysis. Like prior studies [5, 6], it concentrates on general stock market price movements. The model and analysis presented, however, extend the insight into general stock market price movements beyond time constrained, chronologically oriented studies [1, 4, 7, 12], through the use of the market cycle time period.

HYPOTHESIS AND DATA

Given that the stock price represents the present value of the future stream of benefits (primarily forecasted through earnings) discounted back to the present by the required rate of return to compensate for the use of money and risk, changes in the price can be directly related to changes in the earnings prospects and in the required rate of return [3]. Changes in the required rate of return for the use of money equate to the nominally observed interest rate consisting of both the real interest rate and the purchasing power, inflation-induced premium. These two factors are the systematic components of the required rate of return. The components of the required rate of return that compensate for individual default and marketability risk associated with the particular security or stock are equivalent to the unsystematic risk and irrelevant to this analysis.

*University of South Florida. The authors wish to thank the reviewers for their helpful comments and suggestions.

As economic activity expands, corporate profits in general accelerate from the trough of the recession, gradually sloping off into a peak as the economy turns down. Interest rates, on the other hand, relatively low and stagnant at the trough, rise as the economy recovers and heads toward the top of the economic cycle. Thus, at the beginning of the recovery low and stable interest rates coupled with rapidly rising earnings expectations force the stock market to turn upward before economic activity. Conversely, at the peak of the economic cycle as earnings prospects are slowing down, rapidly rising interest rates, reflecting potential economic overheating, force the stock market down in general before economic activity peaks. The relationship between these two factors over the entire cycle dictates the pace at which stock prices rise and fall.

The hypothesis tested in this study is that between the low and high of the general market index, as measured by the Standard and Poor's 500 (SP500), and again between the high and the low of the market, there is an inverse relationship between the percentage changes in security prices and in interest rates and a direct relationship between the percentage changes in security prices and in corporate profits, as shown in Equation (1).

$$\%\Delta\ \text{SP500} = \alpha + B_1\ (\%\Delta\text{LTINT}) + B_2\ (\%\Delta\text{PFT}) + e \tag{1}$$

where

$\%\Delta\text{LTINT}$ = percent change in long term yield to maturity on government bond index at half cycle points in SP500

$\%\Delta\text{PFT}$ = percent change in aggregate after tax corporate profits at half cycle points in SP500.

The hypothesized relationships are

$$B_1\ < 0$$
$$B_2\ > 0$$
$$|\ \hat{B}_1\ | = |\ \hat{B}_2\ |$$

The data are reported in the Federal Reserve Bulletin. The dates of the observed data are congruent to the highs and lows in the Stan-

Table 1
Results of Equation (1)

	Regression Coefficients			
Constant = 26.4285				
Variable	Coefficient	Beta	F-Ratio	Standard Error
%ΔLTINT	−1.5162	−0.4144	4.153	0.7440
%ΔPFT	1.6411	0.7306	12.907	0.4568

Additional Results

				Adjusted
Coefficient of multiple determination		=	0.5684	.5055
Coefficient of multiple correlation		=	0.7539	.7110
Standard error of multiple estimate		=	38.2919	42.2984

F-Ratio (2,11) = 7.2442
Durbin-Watson statistic = 2.8210
Number of valid cases = 14

dard and Poor's 500 Index from 1964–1983. The half cycle points are determined by plotting the SP500 over the entire time period 1964–1983 and noting the peaks and troughs. The half cycle time period is the time period from peak to trough or from trough to peak on the SP500.

RESULTS

The empirical results reported in Table 1 support the hypothesis. The F-Ratio for the entire equation is significant at the 1% level. Each of the independent variables is also highly significant. The corporate profit percentage change variable is significant at the 1% level in direct relationship. The percent change in the long term interest rate variable is significant at the 6.4% level in inverse relationship. As hypothesized, the corporate profit variable has a coefficient approximately equal in an opposite direction to that of the coefficient for the long term interest rate percent change variable. This implies that the two factors exert almost equal impact over the cycle, and at turning points where the percentage change in one variable exceeds the other, that variable will dominate, causing the turn. At the low, interest rates are stable while earnings prospects spurt causing stock prices to rise. At the high, earnings prospects stagnate while interest rates spurt causing the decline in stock prices. An additional interesting result is the coefficient of multiple determination of 56.84% (adjusted R^2 = 50.55%). This is higher than that observed in some asset pricing model studies. However, about half of the movement in the market is not explained. This large unexplained portion may be due to the differing movements between the risk premium on government bonds and the risk premium in the common stock markets.

The model has made a contribution in explaining the stock market cycles in broad terms with dynamic implications. It has observed and explained to a larger than usually observed degree the stock price movements over time horizons that are compatible with the SP 500 cycle rather than arbitrarily forcing compliance to a calendar definition. The model has further expanded the knowledge of the market movements beyond equilibrium within the market itself to an arena of the entire market.

CONCLUSIONS AND IMPLICATIONS

The way is now open for portfolio managers wishing to engage in active portfolio management on a broad market timing basis to understand the dynamics exposed in this paper. A portfolio strategy based upon active switching techniques can be employed to capture, with limited transactions, movements of security prices which generally account for approximately 50% or more of all price movements.

Although most market observers speak of managing portfolios for consistently profitable long run returns, rewards to portfolio managers are usually geared to short run, calendar specific returns. This model provides a more appropriate comparative base for evaluating portfolio performance. Those managers who are successful in bull markets may not do as well in bear markets. This model enables a comparison of bull and bear market performance regardless of the time span they cover. Furthermore, an effective portfolio manager may have to forego returns in one period to produce excess returns in a later period. The model analyzes the full cycle regardless of the number of months (quarters) involved.

The model explains the majority of the stock market movements without the dangers of individual stock risks and complications from unstable betas or from market shifts disrupting price forecasts because of radical changes in price/earnings ratios. This explanation of market dynamics is not based strictly upon comparative statics resulting from changes in the risk-free interest rate as the only source of broad market movements as in the capital asset pricing model. This explanation of general market movements complements the market-internal equilibrating mechanism.

REFERENCES

[1] Bernstein, P. L. "Markowitz Marked to Market." *Financial Analysts Journal* (January–February 1983): 18–22.

[2] Blume, M. E. "On the Assessment of Risk." *Journal of Finance* (March 1971):1–10.

[3] Bolten, S. E. "Stock Price Cycle Exegesis." *Financial Planning* (December 1985):208–209.

[4] Chance, D. M. "Evidence on a Simplified Model of Systematic Risk." *Financial Management* (Autumn 1982): 53–63.

[5] Farrar, D. E. "The Investment Decision Under Uncertainty." Englewood Cliffs, NJ: Prentice-Hall dissertation series, 1962.

[6] King, B. F. "Market and Industry Factors in Stock Price Behavior." *Journal of Business* (January 1966, supp.):139–170.

[7] Logue, D. E. and Merville, L. J. "Financial Policy and Market Expectations." *Financial Management* (Summer 1972):37–44.

[8] Roll, R., and Ross, S. A. "An Empirical Investigation of the Arbitrage Pricing Theory." *Journal of Finance* (December 1980):1073–1104.

[9] Roll, R. and Ross, S. A. "The Arbitrage Pricing Theory Approach to Strategic Portfolio Planning." *Financial Analysts Journal* (May–June 1984):14–26.

[10] Sharpe, W. F. "A Simplified Model for Portfolio Analysis." *Management Science* (January 1963):277–293.

[11] Sharpe, W. F. "Capital Asset Prices: A Theory of Market Equilibrium Under Conditions of Risk." *Journal of Finance* (September 1964):425–442.

[12] Sharpe, W. F. and Cooper, G. M. "Risk-Return Classes of New York Stock Exchange Common Stocks, 1931–1967." *Financial Analysts Journal* (March–April 1972):46–54 and 81.

Long-Term Asset Allocation under Dynamic Interaction of Earnings and Interest Rates

Steven E. Bolten and Scott Besley*

ABSTRACT

The interaction of interest rates and corporate earnings over the economic cycle generates stock price movements. These movements are captured in the present valuation context. Superior returns are observed when long-term asset allocation techniques are applied to the model.

INTRODUCTION

This research shows that asset allocation among stocks, long-term U.S. Treasury bonds (T-bonds), and Treasury bills (T-bills) based on economic conditions can improve upon buy/hold investment strategies [1, 4–6]. Previous research [2, 3] on stock market cycles suggests that interactive changes in corporate profits and interest rates over the economic cycle have opposite effects on stocks and bonds prices. As a result, an asset allocation strategy using percentage changes in interest rates and corporate profits did, in fact, produce superior returns.

DATA

The quarterly Standard & Poor's 400 Industrial Index (S&P 400 Index), its earnings per share, and its dividends constituted the data for stock and earnings calculations. The S&P 400 Index was chosen because its large portion of industrial company stocks generally are considered a good reflection of economic cycles. The bond prices and interest rates used were the 30-year U.S. T-bond. These were chosen to reflect only interest rate changes and to avoid possible default risk

*University of South Florida, Tamps. FL 33620. The authors thank an unknown reviewer for helpful comments.

Table 1
Market Highs and Lows

Year	Quarter	S&P 400 Index
1967	1	L/ 96.71
1968	4	H/113.02
1970	2	L/ 79.89
1972	4	H/131.87
1974	3	L/ 71.01
1976	3	H/119.46
1978	1	L/ 98.02
1980	4	H/154.45
1982	2	L/122.42
1983	2	H/189.98
1984	2	L/174.73
1987	3	H/375.85
1989	3	397.85

distortions. The 90-day T-bill interest rate was used for short-term rates. The stock market highs and lows were determined using the S&P 400 Index (Table 1).

METHODOLOGY

Four distinct investment strategies were simulated from the end of 1967 to the fourth quarter of 1987. The first study assumed a buy/hold for the S&P 400 Index. The second strategy assumed a buy/hold for the 30-year T-bonds. The third strategy assumed a buy/hold of the T-bills reallocated every 90 days. The fourth strategy assumed a quarterly asset allocation based on equation (1).

The S&P 400 Index buy and hold strategy over the 20-year period, reinvesting all dividends, resulted in an average 10.6 percent yearly return. The T-bill strategy, reinvesting interest in capital gains, resulted in a 6.1 percent average return. The buy/hold investment strategy for the 30-year U.S. T-bonds, including quarterly reinvestment of interest, resulted in a 7.8 percent yearly average return.

The asset allocation strategy, with quarterly reallocation between stocks and long-term bonds, resulted in a 12.9 percent annual return. The reallocation between the two was based on the percentage increase or decrease in the S&P 400 Index earnings and in the interest rates on long-term bonds. The percentage change in the earnings of the prior quarter of the S&P 400 Index, minus the percentage change in the long-term bond interest rate of the prior quarter resulted in a combined change of the two or, as we will call it, a total change:

$$\text{Total change} = \%\Delta E - \%\Delta i \qquad\qquad (1)$$

where

$\%\Delta E$ = prior quarter percent change in earnings,

$\%\Delta i$ = prior quarter percent change in 30-year T-bond yields.

The reallocation at the beginning of each quarter was based on the prior quarter's total change in equation (1).

As the expansionary part of the business cycle propels earnings upward more rapidly than interest rates, total change is positive, and money is shifted from stocks to bonds. This reallocation continues every quarter in proportion to the total percentage change observed. Reported data on earnings and dividends were not available at more frequent intervals.

Ideally, when the percentage change in earnings growth exactly equals the percentage change in interest rates, the portfolio is entirely in bonds because equities have peaked. The reverse portfolio reallocation starts with earnings declining but interest rates declining more rapidly. The result is a negative total percentage change and a shift from bonds to stocks. This captures the dynamic interaction of earnings and interest rates in the present discounted value model of stock prices [2].

The reallocation between stocks and bonds is based solely on the prior quarter's reported percentage change in earnings and interest rates in equation (1). This reallocation method outperformed the market over the period used in the study. This result was found for both the long-term, original sample and the shorter-term, out-of-sample test. Even though this is a total cycle, the longer-term model and the out-of-sample results were only for two years in a bull market environment, the asset allocation was superior to the buy/hold strategies for stocks and about equal to the bonds, which historically have produced spurts of short-term superior return as in this sample. With perfect hindsight, a 100 percent switching from stocks at the equity highs into T-bills then into bonds at the peak in economic activity and back into stocks at the market lows had the highest return, 15.7 percent before commissions, as expected from hindsight. The 12.9 percent pre-commission return is not based on hindsight and still outperforms the buy and hold of stocks, T-bills, or long-term T-bonds by themselves. We suggest that the 100 percent hindsight model cannot be implemented and recommend the asset allocation strategy based on the total percentage change indicator of equation (1).

The asset allocation model, which produced superior returns, may have lower risk. We are dealing only with systematic risk in stocks by using the S&P 400 Index. Intuitively, we cannot reduce the systematic stock risk; it is already a fully diversified portfolio of 400 stocks. We have no default risk in the U.S. government securities, the other assets.

The risk is a short-term, large whipsaw move in the assets' prices from quarter to quarter, not in the traditional systematic or unsystematic measures of risk. Fortunately economic cycles for which this allocation strategy is designed tend not to whipsaw so dramatically. The model is designed as a long-term portfolio strategy over the entire cycle including recession and expansion.

TRANSACTIONS COSTS

The transactions costs associated with this asset allocation strategy are relatively low. These low transactions costs are the natural result of reallocation only quarterly, the homogeneity of the securities used, the efficiency of financial markets, the mechanical nature of the allocation rules, and the ready availability of noload S&P Index and U.S. T-bond mutual funds with switching privileges.

The S&P Index and the U.S. Treasuries used in the allocation are homogeneous securities offered by several low-cost providers such as Vanguard. Many have historically closely tracked the securities. Demand will naturally move toward the least cost provider in an efficient market of homogeneous products. The impact of transactions costs will therefore approximate the administrative costs borne by investors in these no-load funds. Applying the observed .25 percent to .50 percent annual expense fee still keeps the return to the asset allocation strategy superior to that of the buy/hold approach.

Often the reallocations are relatively small as called for by the total percentage change in equation (1). The impact of transactions costs on the annual return would be modest.

All but the largest investors might use no-load index or other mutual funds switching techniques at no transactions costs. They would bear management and administration fees. The largest investors typically negotiate relatively low commissions.

CONCLUSIONS

Based solely on the historical percentage change in earnings and interest rates in the prior quarter, the asset allocation strategy produced a 12.9 percent return. The asset allocation model based on the total change indicator of equation (1) is suggested as an appropriate portfolio management tool for achieving potentially superior returns. This was above the stock buy/hold strategy return of 10.6 percent for the first quarter of 1967 through the fourth quarter of 1987. We conclude that dynamic asset allocation based on the interactive movements of earnings and interest rates is a viable technique for potentially superior investment performance.

REFERENCES

[1] Admati, Anat R., Sudipto Bhattacharya, Paul Pfleiderer, and Stephen A. Ross. "On Timing and Selectivity." *Journal of Finance* 41 (July 1986): 715–732.

[2] Bolten, Steven E. "Cycle Exegesis." *Financial Planning* (November 1985): 208–210.

[3] Bolten, Steven E., and Susan W. Long. "A Note on Cyclical and Dynamic Aspects of Stock Market Price Cycles." *The Financial Review* 21 (February 1986):145–150.

[4] Farrell, James L., Jr. "A Fundamental Forecast Approach to Superior Asset Allocation." *Financial Analysts Journal* 45 (May/June 1989):32–37.

[5] Ferguson, Robert. "How to Beat the S&P 500 (Without Losing Sleep)." *Financial Analysts Journal* 42 (March/April 1989):37–46.

[6] Perold, Andre F., and William F. Sharpe. "Dynamic Strategies for Asset Allocation." *Financial Analysts Journal* 44 January/February 1988): 16ff.

A Note on the Price Earnings Multiple

Steven E. Bolten, Ph.D., CBA

Price/Earnings (P/E) ratios are used extensively in valuation when publicly held comparable firms are used for their valuation indications. The behavior of the price/earnings multiple is an important, necessary insight for business appraisers. This article shows that the price/earnings multiple is the reciprocal of the required rate of return when earnings are constant. However, when earnings fluctuate the price/earnings multiple tends to be at least temporarily higher for growth companies during their accelerated growth, countercyclically higher for a cyclical company, and meaningless for companies with current losses. These P/E characteristics arise because the price reflects the entire future stream of anticipated benefits while the earnings used in the computation of the price/earnings multiple is primarily a relatively concurrent one which will not necessarily reflect the entire future prospects for the company.

"The stock market rose today as P/E Multiples expanded, analysts said." (Radio report on the stock market)

The price earnings multiple has considerable importance. It is sufficiently well recognized on a practical application basis that it is reported daily in each of the major financial newspapers. Yet, its fluctuations, independent of constant earnings, are not always clearly understood.

CONSTANT EARNINGS

The share price is the present discounted value of the future stream of dividends implied in earnings. Equation 1 is the value of a stream of future benefits.

$$P_0 = \sum_{t=0}^{\infty} \frac{\hat{E}_t(1 - \lambda)}{(1 + r)^t} \tag{1}$$

P_0 = current share price

$\hat{E}_t$ = forecasted earnings per share in year t

λ = a constant retention rate

r   = required rate of return

Assuming constant earnings, we concentrate solely on the change in the price earnings multiple without regard for the impact of earnings fluctuations. This isolation on the PE multiple is embodied in the PE valuation model ($P/E \times E = P_0$). The share price can change either because the PE changes or the earnings (E) change, or both.

Share price may also be expressed as the sum of a geometric progression:

$$P_0 = \frac{E_1}{(1 + r)^1} + \frac{E_2}{(1 + r)^2} + \cdots \frac{E_n}{(1 + r)^n} \qquad (2)$$

where $E_1 = E_2 = E_n = E$

$$(1 + r) P_0 = E + \frac{E}{(1 + r)^1} + \frac{E}{(1 + r)^2} + \cdots \frac{E}{(1 + r)^{n - 1}} \qquad (3)$$

Subtracting equation (2) from equation (3) we get

$$(1 + r) P_0 - P_0 = E - \frac{E}{(1 + r)^n} \qquad (4)$$

$$rP_0 = E - \frac{E}{(1 + r)^n} \qquad (5)$$

As $n \to \infty$

$$rP_0 = E \qquad (6)$$

and

$$\frac{P_0}{E} = \frac{1}{r} \qquad (7)$$

The PE is the reciprocal of the required rate of return. It is also the cost of equity capital when earnings are held constant.

The PE changes independently of earnings as r, a function of interest rates and other risks, changes. Thus, PE multiples and share prices "expand" or "contract" even when the earnings are constant.

GROWING EARNINGS

The high price earnings multiples of a growth company similarly arise from the same framework. The growth company share price is the present value of the future stream of growing earnings and their implied dividends. The price reflects the entire, infinite horizon of anticipated benefits implied in the future earnings, discounted back to the present. The PE ratio, however, uses only the annual earnings for a relatively concurrent period. A distortion occurs. The price reflects the entire future stream of implied benefits, but is compared only to the current, obviously lower but expected to grow, earnings. This creates a high PE ratio for growth companies.[1]

CYCLICAL EARNINGS

Cyclical companies' share prices appear to vary inversely with their earnings. When the earnings are low during a recessionary period, the PE ratio is higher than when the earnings are high during an expansionary period. Again, there is distortion. The share price reflects the entire, infinite time horizon, while the PE ratio uses a concurrent or near term annual earnings for the denominator. The concurrent earnings are high in an expansion. Yet, the share price reflects the expected, subsequent recessionary decline in earnings. This time horizon distortion causes the share price not to rise proportionately with the observed rise in near term earnings expectations. The price reflects the stream of future, fluctuating earnings, probably reflecting more of a cyclical average. The distortion also occurs at the upper end of the expansion when the price includes the future recessionary expectations while the concurrent earnings do not. This causes a very low PE ratio for a cyclical company in an expansionary period. Conversely, there is a relatively high PE ratio during a recessionary period when the price reflects the future earnings recovery, but the PE ratio still has concurrently depressed earnings in the denominator.[2]

NO EARNINGS (LOSS)

The PE is "not meaningful" when the company has an earnings loss. A negative PE is not logical. The negative earnings in the denominator cause this distortion. The share price reflects the entire future earnings stream even many years ahead when the earnings may recover. The distortion of the concurrent year deficit in the denominator of the PE ratio is a temporary phenomenon.[3]

CONCLUSIONS AND IMPLICATIONS

The share price can fluctuate even with constant earnings because the PE itself moves independently of the earnings. The PE is the reciprocal of the required rate of return. We can appreciate the impact on stock prices of interest rates' fluctuations, such as occurred in 1981 and 1987. In 1987, even though the economy did not fall apart and earnings actually continued to expand, share prices in the crash of October, 1987, fell precipitously. Declining PE ratios accounted for much of the fall.

ENDNOTES

(1) $$P_0 = \sum_{t=0}^{\infty} \frac{\hat{E}_t (1 - \lambda) (1 + g)^t}{(1 + r)^t}$$

g = constant growth rate

$E_0 < E_1 < E_2 < E_3 < E_4$, etc.

$P_0 < P_1 < P_2 < P_3$, etc.

$\dfrac{P_{t+1} - P_t}{P_t} < \dfrac{E_{t+1} - E_t}{E_t}$, etc.

$\dfrac{P_0}{E_0} > \dfrac{P_1}{E_1} > \dfrac{P_2}{E_2} > \dfrac{P_3}{E_3} > \dfrac{P_4}{E_4}$, etc.

(2) $P_0 = \dfrac{E_1 (1 - \lambda)}{(1 + r)^1} + \dfrac{E_2 (1 - \lambda)}{(1 + r)^2} + \dfrac{E_3 (1 - \lambda)}{(1 + r)^3}$ /

$\qquad + \dfrac{E_4 (1 - \lambda)}{(1 + r)^4} + \ldots + \dfrac{E_n}{(1 + r)^n}$

$E_0 < E_1 > E_2 < E_3 > E_4 \cdots E_n$

$E_t = E_{t + 2}$ and $E_{t + 1} = E_{t + 2}$

$n = \infty$

$\dfrac{\sum\limits_{t=0}^{n} E_t}{n} = \bar{E}$

$P_0 = \sum\limits_{t = 1}^{n} \dfrac{\bar{E}_t (1 - \lambda)}{(1 + r)^t}$

$\dfrac{P_0}{E_0} > \dfrac{P_1}{E_1} < \dfrac{P_2}{E_2} > \dfrac{P_3}{E_3} > \dfrac{P_4}{E_4}$, etc.

(3) $P_0 = \sum\limits_{t = 1}^{\infty} \dfrac{\hat{E}_t (1 - \lambda)}{(1 + r)^t}$

$E_0, E_1 < 0$

$\quad E_2, \cdots, E_\infty > 0$

$P_0 > 0$

$E_0 < 0$

$\dfrac{P_0}{E_0}, \dfrac{P_1}{E_1}, < 0$, not meaningful

$\dfrac{P_2}{E_2}, \cdots, \dfrac{P_\infty}{E_\infty} > 0$

Time Horizon Premiums as a Measure of Stock Market Bubbles

Steven E. Bolten, Ph.D., ASA, CBA

ABSTRACT

This research observes unusually large lengthening or shortening in the duration of investors time horizons at stock market bubbles shortly before they burst. This has occurred at every bubble in the last 32 years for which the data was tested.

INTRODUCTION

The value of a stock or collectively the stock market is the present value of the anticipated future stream of benefits to be received. [4] The current dividend is usually less than that of the yield to maturity on the long-term U.S. Treasury bond. This observed difference in value between the certain stream, such as that of the long U.S. Treasury bond, and the uncertain, variable stream, such as that of a common stock, must be made up in growth to compensate for the additional risk. In other words, the required risk premium to the common stock is reflected in investors' collective judgment of the growth. If the anticipated growth fails to materialize, the stock valuation must decline to bring the required return into alignment. The converse occurs when the stock market is collectively so pessimistic that it overly discounts or ignores the growth prospects. When the growth does materialize, the stock valuations must then rise. [3]

At any given growth rate, the anticipated duration of that growth must be sufficient to close the gap between the present value of the certain and the uncertain streams. As the anticipated duration increases, the stock value also increases. The risk, too, increases, because there is a more protracted period during which the assumed, given growth rates may not be realized. If this occurs, stock market valuations fall.

If we can observe the implied growth duration, we can get a feel for the over or under optimism of the stock market. High, anticipated growth duration implies higher risk and may be associated with the relatively infrequent, but large stock market bubbles and subsequent bursts, which have occurred within the last thirty years or so.

We believe we have observed this relationship between overly high or low, anticipated growth duration and stock market bubbles and recoveries.

ANALYTICAL FRAMEWORK

The gap between the actual stock price (S) and its theoretical, no growth, risk free value (S_{ng}) is:

$$S - S_{ng}$$

S_{ng} is calculated as:

$$S_{ng} = \sum_{t=1..\infty} Et\ (p)/(1 + r)^t$$

Where

E_t is the anticipated no growth future benefits stream from earnings

p is the constant earnings payout percentage

r is the no growth, risk free, long-term U.S. Treasury bond yield to maturity

We can, assuming equal, long-term infinite time horizons for both the stocks and the long-term Treasury bond that the no growth stock present value is

$$S_{ng} = E(p)/r$$

S_{ng} must increase in price to equal S in order for the stockholder to be compensated for the implied risk premium. This is only done through the growth in the earnings.

If we take the observed implied future growth (g) and determine the number of years (n) it would take at that growth rate to get $S = S_{ng}$, we can judge the exuberance (or pessimism) embedded in the stock market valuations. A large positive n implies large confidence, which pushes the market to higher valuations and exposes it to a greater possibility of disappointment, initiating stock price declines.

Conversely, a large negative n implies low confidence, which pushes the stock market to lower valuations and exposes it to a greater possibility of recovery.

EMPIRICAL TESTING

1. We computed S_{ng} as the capitalized valuation of the Standard and Poor's Industrial Index earnings. We used the three quarters leading S&P Industrials earnings to reflect the discounting, anticipatory nature of the stock market. Also, the smallest gap between the no growth and the actual index was observed from among those tested. We wanted to work with the smallest gap. The data spanned the first quarter of 1966 to the first quarter of 1997.

2. We used the BBB long-term bond yield to maturity to extract some of the risk premium over the U.S. Treasury bond yield. This left more emphasis on the growth in the risk premium. Also, the BBB capitalized based was the closest to the observed S&P Industrial Index.

3. The time horizon risk premium (n) reflects the number of years it would take at the observed rate of growth, judged by the historic growth in earnings over the last three quarters, to close the gap between S and S_{ng}. We took the percentage by which S exceeded or fell short of S_{ng} and calculated how many years it would take at that growth rate to close the gap. The average time horizon risk premium was 1.54 years. The median was .98 year, which finds support in the myopic results of earlier studies [2].

When n is a very large positive or negative, we have an over or under enthusiasm bubble indication.

RESULTS

We can see from Exhibit 1 that every time but one in the last 32 years, when n became very large, this indicated a bubble and the stock market fall or rose shortly thereafter.

In the third and fourth quarters of 1993, n was 17.31 and 25.36, respectively. The S&P Industrial Index subsequently fell. The time horizon risk premium (n) returned to more normal levels and stock market valuations recovered.

In the fourth quarter of 1987 and the first quarter of 1988, n fell to extremely low levels of −12.27 and −74.62, respectively. The time

Exhibit 1

SP Ind	Nyrs	Date	SP Ind	Nyrs	Date	SP Ind	Nyrs	Date
1194.97		3/98	234.56	1.05	4/85	125	-1.42	1/73
1333.54		2/98	203.67	0.98	3/85	131.87	46.62	4/72
1282.23		1/98	211.92	0.83	2/85	123.74	5.21	3/72
1121.38	0.94	4/97	201.67	0.76	1/85	119.91	2.22	2/72
1108.37	0.94	3/97	186.36	0.73	4/84	119.26	1.61	1/72
1042.97	0.94	2/97	187.41	0.82	3/84	112.72	1.37	4/71
889.26	0.96	1/97	174.73	1.04	2/84	108.77	1.46	3/71
869.97	1.14	4/96	180.14	1.69	1/84	109.95	1.34	2/71
812.85	1.72	3/96	186.24	3.75	4/83	110.42	1.34	1/71
796.36	2.13	2/96	187.38	9.84	3/83	100.9	1.17	4/70
761.8	1.93	1/96	189.96	4.11	2/83	92.57	0.96	3/70
721.19	1.18	4/95	171.65	1.84	1/83	79.89	0.81	2/70
686.52	0.85	3/95	157.62	1.16	4/82	98.05	0.79	1/70
649.66	0.83	2/95	134.45	0.78	3/82	101.49	0.82	4/69
596.69	1.02	1/95	122.42	0.71	2/82	102.49	0.81	3/69
547.51	3.14	4/94	124.23	0.66	1/82	107.06	0.87	2/69
548.18	-2.96	3/94	137.12	0.71	4/81	110.91	0.96	1/69
516.4	-1.30	2/94	130.04	0.79	3/81	113.02	1.12	4/68
521.16	-0.94	1/94	147.58	0.94	2/81	112.01	1.24	3/68
540.19	25.36	4/93	164.19	1.25	1/81	108.31	1.40	2/68
516.72	17.31	3/93	154.45	1.11	4/80	98.2	5.84	1/68
514.26	1.87	2/93	142.82	1.16	3/80	105.11	1.64	4/67
517.69	1.21	1/93	128.34	-1.90	2/80	105.05	2.02	3/67
507.46	1.02	4/92	115.31	0.32	1/80	97.71	3.38	2/67

146

490.49	0.98	3/92	121.02	1.11	4/79	96.71	0.08	1/67
480.31	1.32	2/92	122.09	0.90	3/79	85.24	4.32	4/66
480.15	1.36	1/92	114.14	0.79	2/79	81.65	1.49	3/66
492.72	1.27	4/91	113.38	0.75	1/79	90.72	1.08	2/66
458.44	0.89	3/91	107.21	0.70	4/78	95.51	0.78	1/66
442.06	0.74	2/91	113.72	0.64	3/78			
444.21	0.68	1/91	105.53	0.66	2/78			
387.42	0.72	4/90	96.02	0.78	1/78			
360.47	0.80	3/90	104.71	0.84	4/77			
420.51	0.90	2/90	106.22	0.87	3/77			
394.18	0.94	1/90	110.72	0.84	2/77			
403.49	0.83	4/89	109.35	0.73	1/77			
397.95	0.82	3/89	119.46	0.55	4/76			
363.48	0.78	2/89	118.07	0.21	3/76			
339.42	0.89	1/89	117.38	-2.65	2/76			
321.26	1.22	4/88	115.06	-0.50	1/76			
311.67	2.23	3/88	100.88	-0.09	4/75			
315.73	4.20	2/88	93.95	0.12	3/75			
300.39	-74.62	1/88	106.86	2.42	2/75			
285.85	-12.27	4/87	93.54	0.35	1/75			
375.85	3.60	3/87	76.47	17.83	4/74			
352.98	11.54	2/87	71.01	1.99	3/74			
335.53	20.01	1/87	97.39	2.62	2/74			
269.93	5.64	4/86	105.08	0.53	1/74			
256.06	1.13	3/86	109.14	0.41	4/73			
279.78	0.96	2/86	121.58	-2.23	3/73			
263.51	0.92	1/86	116.72	-0.44	2/73			

horizon risk premium (n) returned to more normal positive levels and the stock market recovered.

In the first and second quarters of 1987, n was 20.01 and 11.54, respectively. The stock market fell in the third quarter and crashed in the fourth quarter of that year.

In the third quarter of 1983, n was 9.84. The market subsequently fell and then recovered along with n returning to more normal levels.

In the fourth quarter of 1974, n was 17.84, but the stock market had already declined after an earlier indication of over exuberance and continued to decline.

In the fourth quarter of 1972, n reached 46.62, and the stock market subsequently declined. Stock valuations stayed down even after n recovered to more normal levels.[1]

CONCLUSION

The stock markets relatively infrequent bouts of over and under enthusiasm can be crudely measured as years of anticipated growth embedded in the risk premium. Extremes in n may be indicative of high-risk periods of impending decline or, in the case of extremely low n, impending market recoveries.

REFERENCES

[1] Bolten, Steven E. and Scott Besley, "The Impact of Seasonality in Earnings Expectations on Stock Prices", *American Business Review*, January, 1993.

[2] Fama, Eugene, *Foundations of Finance: Portfolio Decisions and Securities Prices*, Basic Books, 1976.

[3] Malkiel, Burton G., "Equity Yields, Growth, and the Structure of Share Prices", *American Economic Review*, December, 1963.

[4] Williams, J. B., *The Theory of Investment Value*, Cambridge, 1938.

ENDNOTES

1. The incidences of bubbles appear most frequently in the third and fourth quarters of the year.

The author wishes to thank Richard Meyer and Sean Murphy for their comments and assistance.

The Influence of Liquidity Services on Beta

Steven E. Bolten and John H. Crockett*

1. INTRODUCTION

Although the relationship between the institutional characteristics in the securities markets and the risk-return characteristics of the traded securities has received substantial attention, a number of issues in this area remain controversial. The resolution of these questions is important in order to increase the likelihood that public policy efforts to modify the functioning of the securities markets, given the objective of increasing the allocational and transactional efficiency of these markets, will achieve desirable results. One of these issues, the subject of this paper, involves the relationship between the availability of liquidity services and share price volatility or systematic risk, as measured by beta.

On the one hand, it has been argued that the availability of liquidity services, measured operationally by the bid-ask spread as a proxy for marketability, is associated with changes in share price volatility. This position has been supported by Tinic and West in discussing the Canadian market [11], by the New York Stock Exchange (cited by Barnea and Logue [1]), and by Wall Street folklore. In contrast, the absence of a relationship between the availability of liquidity services and share price volatility has been noted by Benston and Hagerman [2] and by West and Tinic for the U.S. markets [12].

One potential source of this conflicting evidence may be in the inability of the capital asset pricing model as it is generally applied to represent adequately the relationship between liquidity services and price volatility. The capital asset pricing model rests on the assumption of perfect markets, where it is supposed that no transactor is sufficiently large relative to the market to influence price volatility through his demands for liquidity services. In markets with significant

*The authors, the University of South Florida and the University of Houston, respectively, are grateful to Charles P. Harper and Edward Liao for suggestions and assistance which have contributed materially to the research reported in this paper.

activity by institutional investors, this condition may be violated. If this were the case, the empirical analysis of beta might be distorted as a consequence of the lack of a framework within which the impact of liquidity services on beta can be identified. Empirically, this possibility corresponds to a misspecification of the return-generating process operating in the institutionally dominated segment of the market.

This paper examines directly the potential impact of the availability of liquidity services on the empirical determination of beta by examining the place of liquidity services in the market model itself. This approach is in contrast to prior studies which obliquely investigate the possible relationship between a liquidity services proxy, the bid-ask spread, and price volatility measures.[1]

In fact, we have also found no evidence of a statistically significant relationship between the bid-ask spread and beta. This finding, however, is not sufficient to justify the inference of independence between beta and the availability of liquidity services. For example, the Smidt "Dynamic Price/Inventory Adjustment Theory," described by Barnea and Logue [1], suggests that the bid-ask spread may remain constant while substantial price volatility occurs if market makers maintain a constant spread while changing both bid and ask prices in response to changing demands for their liquidity services. As a result, the absence of a correlation between the absolute spread and beta may not accurately reflect the lack of a liquidity service impact on beta.[2] To identify such an impact, it is necessary to integrate the role of liquidity service directly into the process of beta determination.

2. A THEORETICAL STATEMENT OF THE PROBLEM

The impact of the availability of liquidity services on price volatility in an efficient market operating as envisaged by the capital asset pricing model can be interpreted in either of two ways. First, it can be argued that the liquidity services impact on share prices is indepen-

---

[1]The New York Stock Exchange study used a ratio of the price range to the low price. The Benston and Hagerman study used a five-year average of beta. Tinic and West employed the standard deviation of security price [12] and the change in price [11].

[2]This is particularly true in instances where absolute bid-ask spread has been used, rather than the bid-ask spread scaled for price levels.

dent of the equilibrium price determined by fundamental risk-return parameters. Beta reflects information excluding liquidity services demands, which are viewed as manifestations of temporary imbalances in supply and demand which do not influence the underlying risk-return factors. In this view, liquidity services demands are treated as random occurrences which cause temporary concentrations on one side of the market, created by the desire for immediate execution of transactions. After the temporary liquidity service demand has been satisfied, the market reverts to evaluation based on the fundamental risk-return parameters. The direct impact of the liquidity service demands on price volatility is temporary and random over many stocks and time periods. It is to be expected that these impacts are distributed evenly around the equilibrium price reflecting the risk-return evaluation. Empirically, the liquidity service impacts wash out in the determination of beta.

Alternatively, the liquidity service impacts might be impounded in beta as an element of marketability risk if the market recognizes this risk. Typically, stocks with small floating supplies, large institutional holdings, and other factors which restrict their marketability are potentially more volatile.[3] The market equilibrium price would then explicitly reflect the potential impact of liquidity services as an element in the basic risk-return information set, even if this impact were expected to occur randomly and temporarily. In short, the marketability risk would be reflected in the expected return as an integral part of price volatility or beta.

In view of these alternatives, the question of primary concern here is whether liquidity services, especially those required by institutions in acquiring and liquidating relatively large positions, affect portfolio betas directly or are random and temporary occurrences independent of portfolio betas. To investigate this issue, we construct tests of the liquidity services impact on a group of sample betas within the capital asset pricing model under each of these alternatives.

Equation 1 summarizes Alternative I. If, as Alternative I suggests, there is an unspecified liquidity services influence L on beta, this influence must be included in the error term when the model is estimated. Part of the error term is thus L, and it must be independent

---

[3]Increased marketability risk leads to a higher ex ante rate of return than would otherwise be expected, although it may lead to a lower than expected ex post holding period return.

of the other components of the model, while being distributed normally with an expected value of zero and a constant variance.[4] If this is not the case, the market model is misspecified with respect to the impact of liquidity services, leading to bias and inconsistency in the coefficients estimated by ordinary least squares.[5]

$$R_j = R_f + \beta_j(R_m - R_f) + (e + L). \qquad (1)$$

In contrast, the approach of Alternative II, suggesting that liquidity services are an integral part of beta, is depicted in Equation II:

$$R_j = R_f + [\beta'_j + f(L_j)] (R_m - R_f) + e. \qquad (2)$$

In this expression, $f(L_j)$ represents a function of liquidity services that is not represented explicitly in the market model but which is in actuality included ex ante in beta by an efficient market. β'_j reflects the influences of all other factors which impact beta.

Notice that if $f(L_j)$ is independent of β'_j as a separate consideration added into beta, ex post betas are expected to be stable only if liquidity services remain constant through time. If $f(L_j)$ does not remain constant, then observed changes in price volatility (beta) are caused in part by a changing market structure (liquidity services), which is typically assumed constant. If $f(L_j)$ is not independent of β'_j but included as part of an overall ex ante beta, group ex post betas should remain stable, despite changes in $f(L_j)$, because the liquidity service considerations are already included in the ex ante risk-return parameters used in beta. In other words, the market model is sufficiently robust to compensate for any changes in $f(L_j)$ for portfolios.

On the other hand, for Alternative I, only if the impact of liquidity services on price volatility is temporary and randomly distributed, with mean zero and constant variance, will the beta estimate not be influenced. In order for the estimated beta to be an accurate predictor of future price volatility, it is necessary that the impact of liquidity

[4]It is highly unlikely that the various liquidity services characteristics used to depict the distribution would be jointly distributed with zero mean and constant variance if none of the individual characteristics was so distributed, but the error term can be tested for zero mean on its own.
[5]If the market model of Equation 1 is misspecified, an additional term is required to represent the influence of liquidity services.

services on price volatility be independent of all other influences on beta and constant over time.[6]

3. THE DATA

To assess the impact of the availability of liquidity services in the market model, two periods were selected for analysis. The periods were May 22, 1970 to April 23, 1971 (the 1971 period) and August 6, 1971 to May 26, 1972 (the 1972 period). These periods were chosen because they represented similar market environments and because they were separated by a period sufficiently long to enable increased institutional demand for liquidity services in the markets for stocks included in the sample. Both periods can be characterized as bullish markets during which institutional holdings increased.

Thirty stocks, listed in Table 1, were chosen at random from the national over-the-counter market. At a later stage of the analysis, data limitations necessitated the elimination of two of the stocks, so that the final sample consisted of 28 securities. Of these, approximately half had some institutional appeal, with 10 percent or more of their shares held by institutional investors. The remainder of the sample was not institutionally oriented during the sample periods.

For each stock, biweekly observations on closing bid and ask prices were made. From these price data, biweekly return figures were calculated by forming price relatives; dividend payments were uniformly ignored. For each security, price volatility or beta was computed by regressing biweekly returns with corresponding returns for a market index, represented by the Standard and Poor's 500. From these regressions, the unexplained variance of the returns was taken as an estimate of each security's unsystematic risk.

The following variables were employed in analyzing the impact of liquidity services availability:

1. the number of institutions holding the stock
2. the number of shares held by institutions
3. the number of shares outstanding
4. the percentage of shares outstanding held by institutions
5. the number of shareholders

[6] This phenomenon would raise particular difficulties in the use of instrumental variables of prior period betas unless liquidity services factors remain constant.

Table 1
Relative Bid-Ask Spreads and Betas

		1971		1972	
A. Institutional Segment					
Stock		Bid-Ask	Beta	Bid-Ask	Beta
Anheuser-Busch		.74%	.68	.89%	1.89
American Express		.76	.68	.70	.01
Southwest Bancshares		3.17	- .13	11.67	.63
Franklin Life Insurance		2.42	1.58	.57	.48
Kaiser Steel		7.57	1.01	3.10	1.91
Mellon National Bank		1.14	.12	.91	.33
A. C. Neilson		2.46	.58	1.27	.58
Pabst Brewing		1.22	.72	.42	1.47
Roadway Express		2.81	.15	1.35	1.99
Stanley Home Products		5.18	- .04	3.36	- .13
Tampax		1.36	.88	7.96	-2.66
U. S. Trucklines		2.27	.34	.47	.28
Yellow Freight		1.94	- .48	2.09	2.97
B. Non-Institutional Segment					
Acme Electric Corporation		11.88	.02	6.80	.01
American Electronic		5.57	1.45	11.07	1.19
American Furniture		7.98	3.71	2.71	-1.06
Baird-Atomic, Inc.		8.06	1.70	5.77	.79
First Boston Corporation		3.23	1.26	1.41	1.94
Foster Grant		3.71	.34	2.01	1.84
Monumental Insurance		2.30	.29	1.48	2.83
Photon		4.38	.22	4.09	1.56
Rotron, Inc.		10.75	1.50	7.83	- .48
Scripto, Inc.		6.18	2.46	4.46	1.69
Southwest Gas Corp.		2.33	.24	4.07	- .05
U. S. Sugar Corp.		5.35	.70	3.68	.43
U. S. Envelope Co.		3.44	- .22	3.33	.78
Washington Natural Gas		2.28	1.28	4.00	- .05
Wellington Management		1.94	- .48	2.09	2.97

Pearson correlation coefficient (56 observations) = 0.0412

6. the number of dealers (market makers)

7. the relative bid-ask spread.[7]

These variables were chosen because they represent institutional concentration, the primary concern in this paper, where the major issue under analysis is the impact of demands for liquidity services on price volatility. Data on trading volume and continuity, occasionally used in similar studies, were not available.

[7]Defined as the ratio of the average biweekly bid-ask spreads over the period to the average price for the period:

4. TESTS

Direct tests of the alternative hypotheses based on regression analysis are not appropriate. With respect to Alternative I, in the standard market model, it would be impossible to reformulate the model to observe directly the effect of the unobserved liquidity services factor apart from the error term. So far as Alternative II is concerned, the critical issue is whether the significant variables representing liquidity services are constant between periods. If not, we are interested in whether these influences are adequately reflected as an ex ante risk consideration in the beta estimate.

Turning now to a detailed analysis of Alternative I, several possibilities for testing the accuracy of the specification embodied in the conventional market model were considered. Since the basic issue involves the possible omission of a relevant explanatory variable, thereby leading to a violation of the Gauss-Markov assumption of a zero mean of the disturbance term, it was decided to test the model as specified to determine whether the specification was consistent with the zero-mean assumption.

Tests of model specification for use in situations such as this have been developed by Ramsey [6]; subsequently the tests were evaluated in a Monte Carlo study by Ramsey and Gilbert [8]. The test employed here was RASET, a test based on Spearman's rank correlation test and not dependent on the presence of normality in the disturbances. The test is implemented by the calculation of a test statistic from the Thiel residuals which under the null hypothesis of zero mean of the disturbances has a t distribution.[8]

Separate regressions of Equation 1 for each of the 28 securities in both sample periods were estimated. Out of the 56 regressions, in only one instance could the null hypothesis of a zero mean of the disturbance term be rejected at the 5 percent level of significance, with 20 observations in the 1971 period and 23 observations in the

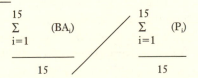

The sources of data used are the following: bid and ask prices were obtained from the *ISL Daily Stock Price Record* [4], variables 1–6 were obtained from the Standard and Poor's *Stock Guide* [10], the number of dealers was obtained from the *National Stock Summary* [5].

[8]The program used in estimating the market model for carrying out the specification error tests was developed by Ramsey [7].

1972 period. In view of the power of the RASET test, these results indicate that a relevant explanatory variable in the form of a liquidity services measure has not been omitted from the market model. Thus, the impact of the availability of liquidity services envisioned by Alternative I must be rejected.

To gain additional insight into the possible influences of liquidity factors on the determination of risk and return characteristics of securities in the sample, some indirect tests were carried out to analyze the stability of the variables under analysis. The procedure followed was to employ a test to determine whether there was a statistically significant difference in the structure of liquidity services between the institutional and the noninstitutional segments of the sample. Additionally, similar tests were utilized to determine which liquidity service variables were significantly different between the periods.

A test of difference between means of each segment was carried out using the Mann-Whitley U test.[9] Although similar in interpretation to the familiar t test between sample means, the Mann-Whitley test is more general in that it does not assume that the samples are drawn from symmetrically distributed populations. Although there is some loss of efficiency as a result of employing testing procedures based on the mean values of variables in each sample segment, the pooling approach was taken in order to minimize the effect of possible measurement error associated with fluctuations in the price volatility of individual securities.

Table 2 summarizes the results of the tests analyzing the differences between the two sets of securities. It is evident from the test on the intersegment relationships that there is in fact a "two-tier" structure of liquidity services. For each time period, the number of institutions holding the stock, the number of shares held by institutions, the number of shares outstanding, the percentage of shares held by institutions, and the relative bid-ask spread were significantly different between the institutional and the noninstitutional segments. The number of market markers was significantly different only in the 1972 period. These results confirm the existence of a segmented demand for liquidity services, in spite of what might be regarded as an imprecise measure for differentiating institutional and noninstitutional stocks.

Table 3 presents results of the tests for time-wise shifts in the

[9]For a description of the Mann-Whitley U test, see Siegel [9], pp. 116–126.

Table 2
Segment Relationships

Variable	U	Significant at 15%
1. Number of institutions holding stock		
1971 NI* V 1971 I	3.5	yes
1972 NI V 1972 I	3.6	yes
2. Number of shares held by institutions		
1971 NI V 1971 I	3.3	yes
1972 NI V 1972 I	3.8	yes
3. Number of shares outstanding		
1971 NI V 1971 I	3.3	yes
1972 NI V 1972 I	3.2	yes
4. Percentage of shares held by institutions		
1971 NI V 1971 I	2.3	yes
1972 NI V 1972 I	3.5	yes
5. Number of shareholders		
1971 NI V 1971 I	1.54	no
1972 NI V 1972 I	1.26	no
6 Number of dealers		
1971 NI V 1971 I	1.03	no
1972 NI V 1972 I	2.12	yes
7. Unexplained variance		
1971 NI V 1971 I	1.03	no
1972 NI V 1972 I	0.12	no
8. Relative bid-ask spread		
1971 NI V 1971 I	3.06	yes
1972 NI V 1972 I	2.51	yes
9. Beta		
1971 NI V 1971 I	1.63	no
1972 NI V 1972 I	0.12	no

*NI = noninstitutional segment
I = institutional segment

Table 3
Relationships Between Periods

Variable	U	Significant at 15%
1. Number of institutions holding stock		
1971 I V 1972 I	.48	no
1971 NI V 1972 NI	.05	no
1971 ALL V 1972 ALL	.83	no
2. Number of shares held by institutions		
1971 I V 1972 I	2.20	yes
1971 NI V 1972 NI	.75	no
1971 ALL V 1972 ALL	1.74	yes
3. Number of shares outstanding		
1971 I V 1972 I	1.72	yes
1971 NI V 1972 NI	2.40	yes
1971 ALL V 1972 ALL	2.91	yes
4. Percentage of shares held by institutions		
1971 I V 1972 I	1.01	no
1971 NI V 1972 I	.98	no
1971 ALL V 1972 ALL	.25	no
5. Number of shareholders		
1971 I V 1972 I	2.28	yes
1971 NI V 1972 NI	2.62	yes
1971 ALL V 1972 ALL	.09	no
6. Number of dealers		
1971 I V 1972 I	3.07	yes
1971 NI V 1972 NI	2.61	yes
1971 ALL V 1972 ALL	3.91	yes
7. Undefined variance		
1971 I V 1972 I	2.41	yes
1971 NI V 1972 NI	1.70	yes
1971 ALL V 1972 ALL	2.69	yes
8. Relative bid-ask spread		
1971 I V 1972 I	2.45	yes
1971 NI V 1972 NI	1.59	no
1971 ALL V 1972 ALL	1.48	no
9. Beta		
1971 I V 1972 I	.94	no
1971 NI V 1972 NI	.34	no
1971 ALL V 1972 ALL	1.48	no

variables of interest within each segment. What is important here is that while the results reveal significant shifts in the liquidity services variables, there is no evidence of associated shifts in beta as evidenced by the significant Mann-Whitley U test. Both segments underwent significant changes with respect to the number of shares outstanding, the number of shareholders, the number of dealers, and the unexplained variance of return. Only the institutional segment changed with respect to the number of shares held by institutions. Despite these shifts in variables representing liquidity services, estimates of price volatility (beta) for both the noninstitutional and the institutional segments as well as the entire sample remained constant, furnishing evidence in support of Alternative II and group beta stability.[10]

The stability of the betas, as a group, between periods, despite changes in the measures of liquidity, was contrary to our intuitive expectations. Apparently, the markets are efficient in digesting information on liquidity service demands within the market model itself, with the two-tier market structure not contributing to beta instability.[11] The explanation for this finding is that betas remain stable despite changes in the structure of liquidity services because these influences are at least partially included in the market's ex ante consideration of risk-return parameters.[12]

5. CONCLUSIONS AND IMPLICATIONS

The analysis indicates that demands for liquidity services figure directly into the assessment of beta. The contrary hypothesis that these demands are temporary or random over institutionally and non-institutionally oriented stocks appears unfounded. Given the evidence supporting the systematic influence of this factor, greater attention is warranted to the market's efficiency in incorporating elements of

[10]There were no significant changes between periods in the number of institutions holding stock and in the percentage of shares held by institutions. If these were the most appropriate liquidity service measures, we expect the ex post beta to remain stable, as it did, in support of Alternative II under the nonindependence assumption.

[11]As a consequence of this finding, the case for separating liquidity services from the equilibrium price may not be as strong as some suggest. However, a beta for an individual stock rather than a portfolio could change significantly between periods in response to change in liquidity conditions.

[12]This result is consistent with Fisher's conclusion that liquidity premiums are included in bond prices[3]. Further, this result does not exclude the possibility that institutional concentration causes higher betas, i.e., more volatility.

price volatility stemming from liquidity services elements into equilibrium price and prevailing beta. In the face of changing demands for liquidity services between the periods analyzed here, beta remained relatively stable. This finding indicates that beta estimation is sufficiently robust to handle changes in the market's liquidity services function, even though such changes are not random or temporary.

One implication which requires further study is the possibility of effects which the misspecification of liquidity services factors may have on inferences about ex ante expectations from ex post data on the capital market line. Part of the difference between the two may arise because of a failure to reflect accurately the influences of liquidity services variables.

A second area for further investigation revealed by the findings reported here involves the issue of identifying the fundamental determinants of a security's systematic risk or beta. As yet, little is known about why various securities exhibit different responsiveness to movements in the market as a whole; this characteristic, defined by beta, has in effect been taken as what might be called a primitive attribute with no behavioral determinants. Further analysis along the lines of this study may provide increased understanding of the process by which risky prospects are priced by furnishing insights into the underlying factors which determine a security's beta.

REFERENCES

1. Barnea, Amir, and Logue, Dennis E. "The Effect of Risk on the Market Maker's Spread," *Financial Analysts Journal*, 31 (November/December 1975): 45–49.
2. Benston, George J., and Hagerman, Robert L. "Determinants of Bid-Asked Spreads in the Over-the-Counter Market," *Journal of Financial Economics*, 1 (December 1975): 353–364.
3. Fisher, Lawrence. "Determinants of Risk Premiums on Corporate Bonds," *Journal of Political Economy* (June 1959): 217–237.
4. *ISL Daily Stock Price Record (OTC)*. New York: Standard and Poor's Corporation.
5. *National Monthly Stock Summary*. New York: National Quotation Bureau, Inc.
6. Ramsey, J. B. "Tests for Specification Errors in Classical Linear Least Squares Regression Analysis," *Journal of the Royal Statistical Society*, Series B, 31, Part 2 (1969): 350–371.

7. Ramsey, J. B. "Program DATGENTH: A Computer Program to Calculate the Regression Specification Error Tests: RESET, WSET, RASET, BAMSET, and KOMSET." Econometric Workshop Paper No. 6704, East Lansing: Michigan State University, revised, July, 1970.

8. Ramsey, J. B., and Gilbert, R. F. "A Monte Carlo Study of Some Small Sample Properties of Tests for Specification Error." Econometric Workshop Paper No. 6813, East Lansing: Michigan State University, 1969.

9. Siegel, Sidney. *Nonparemetric Statistics*, New York: McGraw-Hill Book Company, 1956.

10. *Standard and Poor's Stock Guide*. New York: Standard and Poor's Corporation.

11. Tinic, Seha, and West, Richard R. "Marketability of Common Stocks in Canada and the U.S.A.: A Comparison of Agent Versus Dealer Dominated Markets," *Journal of Finance*, 29 (June, 1974): 729–746.

12. West, Richard R., and Tinic, Seha M. *The Economics of the Stock Market*, New York: Praeger Publishers, 1971.

The Impact of Management Depth on Valuation

Steven E. Bolten, Ph.D., ASA, CBA and Yan Wang

INTRODUCTION

It is intuitively obvious and frequently observed, but not heretofore quantified, that the lack of management depth is a risk which can impact firm valuation. We quantified the impact of this risk using the analogous methodology applied in judging the impact of control premiums which observe the change in stock prices before and after the merger or acquisition announcement.

THE DATA

We examined the "Who's News" columns of the *Wall Street Journal* from August 1, 1996 through November 28, 1996 for announcements of senior management changes above the rank of vice-president. We selected all that had distinct changes in senior persons with clear indications of policy power. We eliminated many internal promotions where little changed in personnel. For example, we excluded announcements where existing management did not change or an additional new position was created with or without a new person added to the senior management team.

We selected 101 observations within our criteria. When the announcement was made after the markets closed we used the opening price of the next trading day.

METHODOLOGY

We observed both increases and decreases in stock prices associated with the announcement of change in senior management. The market viewed some changes as favorable and others as unfavorable. We all know that good management can take a bad situation and make it good. Bad management can take a good situation and make it bad. We had to split the increase and decrease responses to avoid the

Exhibit 1

SUMMARY				
	Avg. Increase %	Avg. Decrease %	Range	Number of Observations
Small Firm (<280 million)	4.900	-8.65	-27 to 20	27
Large Firm (>=280 million)	2.260	-4.83	-26 to 11	74
By Number of Management				
Less Than 6	8.500	-9.43	-23 to 24	20
Between 6 to 10	2.700	-8	-14 to 23	52
Between 11 and 15	1.180	-3.825	-6 to 14	13
More Than 16	2.342	-2.65	-4 to 19	10
				6 N/A
By Reasons				
Resigned or Step Down	10	-5.67	-6 to 20	39
Replaced or Fired	14.8	-0.69	-0.69 to 15	5
Moved up Internally	8	-5.88	-6.3 to 12	28
Succeed Previous CEO (outsider)	1.25	-5.98	-11 to 7.8	17
Health Problem	2.15	-10.71	-10.7 & 2.15	3
				9 N/A

arithmetic distortion of their offsetting effects on the averages. The risk of management disruption is our concern in the smaller, closely held firms, so it is the average decrease we are most interested herein.

We stratified the sample by size based on capitalization below and above $280 million and, more importantly, on the number of senior management as listed in the Compact Disclosure data base. The latter was stratified as fewer than six; six to ten; eleven to fifteen; and more than fifteen.

We also extracted the reported reason for the management change which we then categorized as: resigned, replaced, moved up internally, succeeded previous CEO (outsider) or health problems.

RESULTS

The results clearly supported the intuitive belief that the departure for whatever reason of a significant key person negatively impacts the firm's valuation (Exhibit 1). On average, the departure of a key management person caused the stock of the smaller, public firms (less than $280 million capitalization) to fall 8.65%. An average negative 4.83% impact was observed for the larger capitalization firms with presumably greater management depth. Of course, we observed increases in the valuation when a perceived favorable change occurred in senior management, as we would logically anticipate.

The smaller firms, where the impact is potentially greater, had the larger observed average percentage change. Since the private firms typically are structured such that the departure of the key person would be negative, the average decrease is typically more significant for the valuation of closely held firms, except in those rare instances where it can be documented that the departure of the key person (usually a family member) may be advantageous. We might add that that is hard to document even in the rare case where it may be true.

The impact of the departure of the key person is increasingly greater as the number of persons on the management team decreases. This observed inverse relationship is, of course, what we would anticipate. With fewer than six persons on the management team, as reported in Compact Disclosure, the average decrease in stock value for the public firm was 9.43%. This result was the highest among the smaller public firms, progressively and consistently rising from −2.65% for firms with more than 16 persons on the management team. We could easily conclude from extrapolation that the negative impact would be even higher for firms with still fewer persons on the management team, such as typically observed in closely held firms. We could not specifically measure the extrapolation because there are no data on those size firms. We notice the analogous impact pattern when the key person change is viewed favorably to the firm.[1]

We also stratified the sample by the market in which the stock was traded as a proxy for liquidity, but the results were about the same regardless of the exchange or market where the stock was traded. The exception was the few foreign traded stocks which showed much larger reactions to the change in key persons.

We also stratified the sample by reasons for leaving, such as health, including death. The results showed no clear pattern that any particular reason caused a greater or lesser impact on the valuation, except for the few, very sudden departures such as unexpected deaths, which caused an over 10% decrease in the valuation.

CONCLUSION

We believe the observed results definitively support the generally accepted assumption that the lack of management depth and the potential loss of a key person(s) negatively impacts valuation. This is particularly true in small, closely held firms where the number of persons on the management team may be as few as one. The degree of negative impact increases as the number on the team decreases. We observed it as high as negative 9.43% for public firms with fewer than six persons on the management team before the lack of data made it impossible to extrapolate any further. However, the negative impact of discount should obviously be higher as the number of persons on the team decreases.

SUMMARY

This research attempts to measure the often observed, but never quantified, risk of lack of management depth on valuation. We observed increasingly larger average declines in the stock prices of public firms accompanying significant management changes as the number of persons on the management team decreases. The stock price decline averages about 9.43% for firms with fewer than six on the management team and probably should be extrapolated higher for smaller firms, although public data was not available for testing.

ENDNOTE

1. The implications, for example, would be an increase in the build-up model. If, everything else constant, a 15% discount rate, not otherwise already considering management depth risk, would increase about 10% for a firm with fewer than 6 on the management team to about 16.5%. In the direct application of our results to the net valuation calculation, a 10% discount would be applied.

Bibliography

Abrams, Jay B. "Discount for Lack of Marketability." *Business Valuation Review* (September 1994).

Ambachtsheer, Keith D. "Pension Fund Asset Allocation: In Defense of the 60/40 Equity Debt Asset Mix." *Financial Analysts Journal* (September/October 1987).

Angell, Robert J., and Alonzo L. Redmon. "Inflation-indexed Treasuries: How Good Are They?" *AAII Journal* (April 1998).

Arnott, Robert D., and James N. von Germeten. "Systematic Asset Allocation." *Financial Analysts Journal* (November/December 1983).

Bendixen, Christian L. "Improved Estimations of Equity Risk Premiums." *Business Valuation Review* (March 1994).

Block, Frank E. "Elements of Portfolio Construction." *Financial Analysts Journal* (May/June 1969).

Bolten, Steven E. "Discounts for Stocks of Closely Held Corporations." *Trusts and Estates* (December 1984).

Bolten, Steven E. "A Note on the Price Earnings Multiple." *Journal of Valuation* (March 1991).

Bolten, Steven E. *Security Analysis and Portfolio Management*. Austin, TX: Holt, Rinehart and Winston, 1972.

Bolten, Steven E., and Robert A. Weigand. "The Generation of Stock Market Cycles." *The Financial Review* (February 1998).

Bolten, Steven E., and Yan Wang. "The Impact of Management Depth on Valuation." *Business Valuation Review* (September 1997).

Bolten, Steven E., and John H. Crockett. "The Influences of Liquidity Services on Beta." *Review of Business and Economic Research* (spring 1978).

Bolten, Steven E., and Scott Besley. "Long-term Asset Allocation under Dynamic Interaction of Earnings and Interest Rates." *The Financial Review* (May 1991).

Bolten, Steven E., and Susan W. Long. "A Note on Cyclical and Dynamic Aspects of Stock Market Price Cycles." *The Financial Review* (February 1986).

Boudoukh, Jacob, Matthew Richardson, and Robert F. Whitelaw. "Nonlinearities in the Relation Between the Equity Risk Premium and the Term Structure." *Management Science* (March 1997).

Brealey, Richard A., and Stewart C. Myers. *Principles of Corporate Finance*. New York: McGraw-Hill, 1996.

Business Valuation Resources, LLC. "New Studies Quantifying Size Premiums Offer Strong Cost of Capital Support." *Shannon Pratt's Business Valuation Update* (August 1997).

Ely, David P., and Kenneth J. Robinson. "The Stock Market and Inflation: A Synthesis of the Theory and Evidence." *Federal Reserve Bank of Dallas Economic Review* (March 1989).

Emory, John D. "The Value of Marketability as Illustrated in Initial Public Offerings of Common Stock (Eighth in a Series) November 1995 through April 1997." *Business Valuation Review* (September 1997).

Fairfield, Patricia M. "P/E, P/B and the Present Value of Future Dividends." *Financial Analysts Journal* (July/August 1994).

Fama, Eugene. *Foundations of Finance: Portfolio Decisions and Securities Prices*. New York: Basic Books, 1976.

Federal Reserve Bank of St. Louis. *Federal Reserve Bank of St. Louis Monetary Trends*.

Fisher, Irving. *The Theory of Interest Rates*. Indianapolis, IN: Macmillan, 1930.

Gilbert, Gregory A. *Handbook of Business Valuation*. New York: John Wiley and Sons, 1992.

Gordon, M. J. "Dividends, Earnings, and Stock Prices." *Review of Economics and Statistics* (May 1959).

Graham, Michael D. "Selection of Market Multiples in Business Valuation." *Business Valuation Review* (March 1990).

Grodinsky, Julius. *Investments*. New York: The Ronald Press, 1953.

Homer, Sidney. *A History of Interest Rates*. New Brunswick, NJ: Rutgers University Press, 1963.

Ibbotson Associates. *Stocks, Bonds, Bills and Inflation, 1999 Yearbook*. Chicago, IL.

Liebowitz, Martin L., and William S. Krasker. "The Persistence of Risk: Stocks versus Bonds over the Long Term." *Financial Analysts Journal* (November/December 1988).

Ma, Christopher K., and M. E. Ellis. "Selecting Industries as Inflation Hedges." *Journal of Portfolio Management* (summer 1989).

Malkiel, Burton G. "Equity Yields, Growth and the Structure of Share Prices." *American Economic Review* (December 1963).

Mercer, Z. Christopher. *Quantifying Marketability Discounts—Developing and Supporting Marketability Discounts*. Memphis, TN: Peabody Publishing, 1997.

Miles, Raymond C. *Basic Business Appraisal*. New York: John Wiley and Sons, 1984.

Pennachi, George G. "Identifying the Dynamics of Real Interest Rates and Inflation: Evidence Using Survey Data." *Review of Financial Studies* (1991).

Perold, Andre F., and William F. Sharpe. "Dynamics Strategies for Asset Allocation." *Financial Analysts Journal* (January/February 1988).

Pratt, Shannon P. *Cost of Capital: Estimation and Applications*. New York: John Wiley and Sons, 1998.

Roll, Richard. "U.S. Treasury Inflation-indexed Bonds: The Design of a New Security." *Journal of Fixed Income* (December 1996).

Schilt, James H. "Selection of Capitalization Rates." *Business Valuation Review* (June 1982).

Schwert, G. William. "Why Does Stock Market Volatility Change Over Time?" *Journal of Finance* (December 1989).

Scott, Maria Crawford. "Asset Allocation Among the Three Major Categories." *AAII Journal* (April 1993).

Siegel, Jeremy J. "The Equity Premium: Stock and Bond Returns Since 1820." *Financial Analysts Journal* (January/February 1992).

Solnik, Bruno. "The Relationship Between Stock Prices and Inflationary Expectations." *Journal of Portfolio Management* (spring 1992).

Swad, Randy. "Discount and Capitalization Rates in Business Valuation." *CPA Journal* (October 1994).

Weston, J. Fred, Eugene F. Brigham, and Scott Besley. *Essentials of Managerial Finance*. Fort Worth, TX: Dryden Press, 1996.

Williams, J. Burr. *The Theory of Investment Value*. Cambridge, MA: Harvard University Press, 1938. Reprint Amsterdam: 1956.

Wrase, Jeffery M. "Inflation-indexed Bonds: How Do They Work?" *Federal Reserve Bank of Philadelphia Business Review* (July/August 1997).

Index

About the Author

STEVEN E. BOLTEN is Professor of Finance at the College of Business Administration at the University of South Florida. He is the author of numerous articles and books. He is an accredited senior appraiser of the American Society of Appraisers, a certified business appraiser in The Institute of Business Appraisers, and frequently consults in business valuation.

ISBN 1-56720-320-5